Becoming Unshakeable

IN A WORLD THAT IS SHAKING

By

Lysa S. Beltz

UNSTOPPABLE
PUBLISHING

Unstoppable Publishing,
231 Public Square, Suite 300
Franklin, TN 37064

To protect the privacy of certain individuals, the names and identifying details have been changed.

Designations used by companies to distinguish their products are often claimed by trademarks. In all instances where the author or publisher is aware of a claim, the product names appear in Initial Capital letters. Readers, however, should contact the appropriate companies for more complete information regarding trademarks and registrations.

"Scripture quotations taken from the Amplified® Bible (AMP), Copyright © 2015 by The Lockman Foundation. Used by permission.www.Lockman.org

Unless otherwise indicated, all Scripture quotations are taken from THE MESSAGE, copyright © 1993, 2002, 2018 by Eugene H. Peterson. Used by permission of NavPress, Represented by Tyndale House Publishers. All rights reserved.

Scripture quotations marked TPT are from The Passion Translation®. Copyright © 2017, 2018 by Passion & Fire Ministries, Inc. Used by permission. All rights reserved. ThePassionTranslation.com.

Cover Design by Klassic Designs, **www.99Designs.com** and Heather Hiatt

Cover images: Earthquake Background - klee048/Shutterstock.com, Black Tree and Roots – rolandtopot/Shutterstock.com, Globe concept tree roots – watchara/Shutterstock.com

Editing by Dana Moon Long, Massive Happiness

ISBN Number: 978-1-7358589-6-8

Printed in the United States of America

Claim your FREE GIFT today!!

Download the companion workbook

(Retails for $22.95 .... Yours FREE!)

As you begin to read Becoming Unshakeable, you are going to want to record all your thoughts and questions and dig deeper. The workbook provides space, prompts, and additional content to help you.

Here's how to access your gift:

1. Go to **www.LysaBeltz.com/gift**
2. Tell us where to email the access link
3. Check your email, then download the PDF
4. Use it right alongside reading the book

Maybe the journey isn't so much about becoming anything. Maybe it's about un-becoming everything that isn't really you, so you can be who you were meant to be in the first place.

-Unknown-

Dedication

This book is dedicated to all those on the highways and bi-ways of life who took an extra right or left turn and ended up out in a field, by yourself, in the dark of night, in a storm. Regardless of how you got there, God's got you! Turn your face towards Him and simply be open to taking one baby step back towards Him and He will make up the entire distance in a single heart-beat.

Life happens. We get to decide if it happens TO us or FOR us. If you are not currently in the driver's seat of your own life, you have the option to change that literally today. If where you are isn't working, change. Ask for help and expect it to arrive. Let me share with you how those changes happened for me and be encouraged by what is possible for you too.

I want to thank several people who helped along my journey. First is my mom who was and will always be one of my heroes. She gave me wings to fly and taught me I could do anything I set my mind to. Next, my husband Scott who has walked with me for 30+ years and been the voice of reason when I was not reasonable. I also want to thank our three daughters; Kelly and Cassie who joined my life as teenagers and our daughter Lindsey, who have all taught me so much in life. I admire you more than you can know. My niece Jinell, for your courage, compassion, and encouragement which came in several forms.

My VBF (Very Best Friend) Shannon whom I've known since first grade. I cannot imagine life without you or your friendship for all these five decades. You will have to always be my best friend – you know where all the proverbial bodies are buried. Much love and appreciation to you.

I also want to thank Natasha Nassar Hazlett and Rich Hazlett for listening to your call and founding Unstoppable Influence. I am not sure this book would be published without you. Thank you for setting the bar high and then empowering me with skills and tools to reach that bar.

What readers are saying about "Becoming Unshakeable"

Becoming Unshakeable is perfect for a new believer or someone more experienced in their journey with God to help take your roots deeper and really make your journey on this earth purposeful and fulfilling!

Jen W.

Becoming Unshakable is a timely read in a tumultuous world. Lysa's faith-based approach to relieving anxiety and redirecting your identity as a child of God is presented in a very simple to understand way. Her take on our connection to our Father God is comforting and beautiful. She puts a unique emphasis on how important it is to feed your spirit. She explains clearly how your spiritual self can grow into relationship with God that produces the peace and confidence needed to maneuver this world. Well written and an easy read, this book encourages you to use your gifts and talents for God's purpose and reminds you of the miraculous relationship you can have with your creator. Each chapter contains thought provoking prompts that assist you with adjusting your focus to get in line with God's will for you. It's truly a game changer.

Karin Kinkade

This book is a wonderful read! Lysa's conversational style draws in the reader as a best friend invites you over for tea and camaraderie. Her message of becoming a strong daughter of God is uplifting and the journal prompts encourage you to stop, absorb and rethink any stale beliefs you may currently hold. I thoroughly enjoyed this novel and encourage all women looking for a close relationship with God to read it!

L. Lyford

Becoming Unshakeable is a fantastic read with a lot of heart. In the weeks and months after reading it, I am still finding new situations to apply the learnings and be a happier, healthier me. I definitely recommend this for anyone looking to start their journey toward being a stronger, smarter woman.

Lindsey Wagstaff

Becoming Unshakeable is transformative and encouraging! The format provides for each person to grow at their own pace and become unshakable in their faith. This book is great for everyone: if you don't know Jesus yet, if you've just met him or if you've had a long journey already knowing the Lord. Becoming Unshakeable will draw you to a deeper, stronger, unshakeable foundation in Him!

Michelle L

The gentle but straightforward style of Lysa's writing feels like a deep conversation over a cup of coffee between old friends. Lysa weaves truth with story in a simple, yet profound way that engages you and encourages you to continue reading. The more that's read, the more that leads to deeper understanding and growth in the relationship with our Creator. There will be laughter, and there may be tears as you read, but there will also be joy and hope."

Dana Long

Table of Contents

Dedication i

What readers are saying about "Becoming Unshakeable" iii

Foreward 2

Introduction 4

Part 1: The Foundation 6

Chapter 1: Who am I? 8

Chapter 2: Who is God, really? 25

Part 2: Becoming Myself 46

Chapter 3: The Destination 47

Chapter 4: Destiny 68

Chapter 5: Obstacles 76

Chapter 6: Choices and Decisions 93

Chapter 7: Any vs. Every Road 103

Chapter 8: Unshakeable Beauty 108

Chapter 9: Abandon the Ugliness 120

Chapter 10: The Yoke 129

Chapter 11: Resilience 136

Chapter 12: Purity of Heart 142

Part 3: Becoming Unshakeable 152

Chapter 13: In Step with the Holy Spirit..............*153*

Chapter 14: Submit and Surrender *163*

Chapter 15: We are an Endangered Species *180*

Chapter 16: Becoming..*195*

Conclusion *216*

Bibliography...*218*

Invitation to Connect *217*

About the Author..*219*

Foreward

There are times that God places someone in your life that has a massive impact on you. That is Lysa for me. I have had the honor of being her Success Coach over the last year and a half. But the funny thing is, she has been who I have needed in my life. There have been countless times that I have said to her...Lysa, I absolutely love the conversations that you and God have with each other. At times I stand in awe of her and the relationship she has with God. I have not been one that has back and forth conversations with God like she does so I find it so fascinating. I have had the joy of watching her write this book and getting to see it come to fruition.

"*Becoming Unshakable*" will take you on an adventure. One where you will want to draw closer to God and what He offers us. As a lifelong believer and follower of Christ, I was blessed with many take-aways from the book. It is written in a way that is easy to read and to follow yet chock full of gold. In each chapter she has "Journey

Milestone" questions for you to answer. Don't skip or skim over them. Take the time to answer the questions, it will help you to go deeper with God. Whether you are a lifelong believer, a new believer, or someone that walked away from God but feels the tug to come back to Him, this book is for you. If you are like me, you will get to the end of the book and want more.

I believe with everything in me that you will be different when you finish reading what God laid on Lysa's heart to share. I hope you will jump in and find your unshakeable faith.

Ronda DeLaughter
Success Coach, Unstoppable Influence
John Maxwell Certified Coach

Introduction

PLEASE READ THIS SECTION

I know most books don't come with instructions, but this
one does. It's a little bit like "some assembly required" (no
batteries needed, however). This is not a book that you will
necessarily have to read from cover to cover although that
approach will work just fine. I think of this as an interactive
book. I have added room in the book for you to jot down
notes and do a little journaling as you hit a section or chapter
that has significance for you. My writing style is
conversational, so I hope it's a little like you and I sitting
down and talking over a cup of coffee or tea as you read this.
Just know that I would thoroughly love to have time to chat
with you!

I have divided the book into three parts. Read *Part One* all the
way through. This lays a foundation for the rest of the
chapters in the book and gives you the background you need
for other ideas to make sense.

Part Two is all about 'Becoming Yourself' and *Part Three* is 'Becoming Unshakable'. These two parts and their associated chapters are where you get to pick and choose how you read them. You may read right through and then find there are chapters or one specific chapter you need to go back and spend time with. There is good information in every chapter, but I encourage you to read where the titles or sub-titles grab your attention. We are attracted to what we need – go with it.

I have been on my own personal journey of releasing man-made religious structures and growing deeper in my relationship with God. I hope that what has taken me decades will take you days or weeks to learn – or more appropriately un-learn.

God gave me the assignment to write this book over 10 years ago. I wrote 3 chapters, then He said I had to go live the rest before I could write the remaining chapters. Had I written the whole book 10 years ago, it would be so different. I have grown so much in the last 2 ½ years and all that would be missed. It really is God's perfect timing that this book is coming to completion now, in 2021.

Part 1: The Foundation

Life is chaotic and unpredictable right now. With a worldwide pandemic, job uncertainties, lots of single parents hustling to provide for their families, national politics that border on bizarre and your own growing-up and becoming process, it gets to be a lot to deal with.

If you are anything like me, you seek authenticity and you want to know you belong to a bigger purpose in life. You are certain there is a Divine Creator, and you'd like to trust and believe that He is on your side. Your childhood memories and experiences with Jesus planted faith and hope and then life happened. Little by little you drifted away from "God" but there is still a knowing that He is there, somewhere. You occasionally pray or think about praying – but, does He even want to hear from you at this point? Is He confused or paralyzed by all the craziness that life has become?

Becoming Unshakeable is a re-introduction to God as Father, Jesus, and the Holy Spirit in a conversational way. It is not about religion or going to church. It is about the heart of God for you. It is about how you are perfectly designed by Him and all the excellence

He sees you with. I hope by the end of your reading that you will genuinely understand how important you are to God and how much He loves and cares for you. Everything that concerns you, concerns Him.

When we have faith in our Creator, we can recognize His goodness in our lives. This includes His acceptance of us regardless of how perfectly imperfect we are and all the stupid things we've ever done. Knowing He loves and welcomes us just as we are, our hope will begin to grow, our self-love and acceptance increases, and faith is reborn. Over time that faith is strengthened again and again until it becomes rock solid. The result of an unshakeable faith will be an unshakeable life.

I strongly encourage you to read all of chapters one and two before you go on to the rest of the book. These two chapters set the foundation and stage that the rest is built on. Spend time here if you need to. There is no race to finish the book – let God show you what you need out of your reading. He knows exactly what will bring your breakthrough and what will give you the peace you need.

Psm 139:
86: 6-8

Psm 91-15
" 100:6

Chapter 1: Who am I?

"The journey of a thousand miles begins with a single step." - Lao Tzu

I am imperfect perfection; a complicated, amazing woman. But who am I really? What makes me, me?

Through the next few chapters, we will break things down a bit and investigate what makes each of us unique and yet, all the same.

We will also look at who God is, how He operates and how we fit with and work with God.

Are we there yet?

My best friend lives a good 7-hour drive away from me. I don't get to see her nearly often enough. We've been friends since the first grade – she's the one who shared Jesus with me and is the friend who has known me the longest. We've been through the tough and lean, the good-bad-and-ugly, and the more carefree times of sleep-overs and dreaming over boys.

When I leave on a trip to her place, it seems to take forever to get there. It's not the journey I look forward to, it's the destination. I have found that life is the same way. However, I get to choose how boring or fun the trip gets to be along the way. It also depends on whether or not I travel alone or someone else comes along for distraction. It can also be affected by how I travel whether in a car or flying on a plane.

My VBF (Very Best Friend) and I have experienced a lot in our years together. We've both had children and now, grandchildren, both experienced divorce but from very different points of view, both had 'careers' that were a bit unexpected, and both have walked with the Lord for the better part of 40+ years and seen Him faithful time and again. In our journeys-to-becoming, our faith has grown, our realism on life has grown, and our love for one another continues to grow year by year. Our journey is a constant, our destination pre-ordained, and our destiny continues to unfold as we become the women we were born to be. Part of this book is based on our experiences and what we've learned along the way.

One of my favorite cartoons of all time is a picture of two guys looking at a snow globe. The first man asks the second,

"How do we know we aren't in someone else's snow globe?" I pondered this question for many years, looking for deeper answers to be sure that life, my life, in particular, had meaning and that it wasn't all just a game of chance. Unshakeable faith will show us where and why we have significance.

When I think about myself, I see a network of relationships, thoughts, activities, desires, fears, hurts, mountains, and valleys, and it gets overwhelming. We are complex creatures as human beings. I am a daughter, a friend, a wife, a mother, an employee, a project manager, a writer, etc. and I am just me. Our lives are so demanding that it is very easy to feel like all I do is spin plates and scramble to keep any of the important ones from crashing and shattering. Is that what God intends for me? Is that really his plan? Intellectually, I don't think so. Spiritually, I know it's not.

Spirit, Soul, and Body

In the many different roles that I fill, I am complicated, and I don't even understand myself sometimes. I know that I am composed of spirit, soul, and body and the Lord made all these pieces to fit together. Spiritually, I'm made up of faith, trust, and belief. My soul is made up of my mind, will, and emotions but I also have conscious, subconscious, and unconscious levels to me. My body has many systems, and I can be weak or strong, healthy or sick in each of those areas. These all interact moment-by-moment in varying degrees of harmony and discord. I war within myself and I get spiritually out of alignment which makes everything run out of sync.

When we get wounded in any of these areas it also affects all of the other parts and pieces. If we have unforgiveness in our spirit, it will impact our physical bodies and cause stress and depression. Each piece is intertwined and cannot be separated. Let's look individually at each of the pieces.

Spirit – our non-physical selves, our innermost being

We are spiritual beings having a human experience. God's word says that even before God created the earth, all of our days were recorded in a book that is kept in the heavenlies. God thought about you, knew about you, and planned for you before He ever created earth and Adam and Eve were formed. Our spirits are eternal. Our spirit was in heaven with Jesus before we were born into the earth to our parents. When we die, our spirit goes to heaven to reunite with Jesus for all of eternity. All of our earthly days were planned out, our gifts, talents, and abilities were given to us, and at the appointed time, we were born into earth's atmosphere to grow, learn, become, and bring glory to God the Father.

Every single person who has ever lived was created with intention by God. There are no mistakes. Period. Every person has a choice of what they do with their life – it is a gift. You have worth and value beyond what you can understand or imagine. Our lives are the currency of heaven. There is no money there – only lives.

In the New Testament scripture of 1 Thessalonians 5:23, it says that we are made the first spirit, then soul, then body – this is God's intended order. Often though, we live body, then soul, and spirit gets last place.

When we ask to have a relationship with God, His Holy Spirit joins with our spirit and we can have continual companionship with Him. We must invite Him in – He will never enter unless we invite Him. Just as a guest would stop at the door to your house and request to come in, the Holy Spirit wants more than anything to be with us. As soon as we open the door to Him, He will flood our spirits with His light and love. It is an amazing experience!

How do you feed your spirit? I'm glad you asked. Every time you read the Word of God (your Bible), you are feeding your spirit. Every time you sing, you feed your spirit. Church services, worship music, spending time with other believers, and being in nature all feed your spirit and can bring growth towards Christ. If only our spirits were as demanding to be fed as our bodies, life would be so different.

In the New Testament, Galatians 5:22 talks about the fruits of the Spirit as love, joy, peace, longsuffering, gentleness, goodness, meekness, temperance, and faith. Participating in activities that stimulate these, feeds your spirit. Living these daily is the outcome of spiritual maturity.

You can feed your spirit junk food, garbage, and harmful substances too; complaining, lacking gratitude, living in fear, hate, continual anger, unforgiveness, gossiping, back-biting, listening to (some) music, and many other things that contribute to a spiritual decline and truly can lead to spiritual and physical death.

Soul - our mind, will, and emotions

Our soul is also known as our psyche. It is our rational <u>mind</u> where we do our thinking, our <u>will</u> where we make choices

13

and decisions, and our emotions where we experience the full gamut of feelings such as love, hate, compassion, joy, anger, or fear. All these together make up our soul or our personality – the 'who we are' part of us.

Before we invite Jesus and the Holy Spirit in, our soul is the primary driver for our decisions. It is where the "If it feels good, do it" mindset comes from. We absolutely can make good soul decisions – but we can make horrible ones, too. Our soul is usually focused on what is good for us and what feels right to us. When you are led by your soul, you can live a good life or a bad life, a moral life or an immoral life, but it is all directed by the soul. We don't often have the discernment or the consideration of God's purpose and plan.

Maya Angelou said, "Do the best you can until you know better. Then when you know better, do better." Until our soul knows there is a different and better way, we do the best we can. Once we encounter God and get into a relationship with Him, we can learn better, and He gives us the ability to do better. God gives us grace – undeserved favor – and that grace will move mountains on our behalf as soon as we set our intention to do better, to follow Jesus.

Body - our physical self

When we are newborns, we cry to be fed, clothed and held. It is our physical needs that cause us to cry out. As we grow older, it is still our physical selves that we experience the most. "I'm hungry, I'm thirsty, I'm too hot, I'm cold, I have to pee." As we all know, our five senses are how we experience the physical world. This physical self is what is visible to others around us and what many of us judge others based on. Our physical body allows us to move about in the earthly realm we live in. God created our physical bodies in His image. In the Old Testament, Psalms 139 says that we are fearfully and wonderfully made.

When I consider just the human eye and the intricacies of how it works, I see how amazing the Creator is with the design of our bodies. Beyond just the eye, all of our systems and how they work and interact together with the intricacies is astounding. We are all complex miracles! In Genesis, Creator God spoke the earth and man into being and He breathed His breath into Adam or none of us would be here.

Achieving Balance

We are three-part beings but there is a connection between

the parts; when you nourish all three in balance, everything in life goes better. We need the balance of all three parts.

➡ If you live in your head, you will be soul-ish and emotional

➡ If you live by your body (flesh), your spiritual heart is neglected

➡ If you only live in the spirit, you are not productive in the world

If you think of concentric circles, our body is the outer circle, soul the middle, and spirit the inner circle:

Figure 1 Spirit, Soul and Body

It's important to also be balanced in nutrition and exercise, mental stimulation, and stress management. We handle life much better when we are eating well and noticing our stress levels. Simply by *choosing* to think differently, we stimulate different neuropathways in our brains and can change the way we think, act, and react to life and stressors.

Journey Milestones:

1. Thinking of where you are in life today, where are you out of sync with yourself? Are you living spirit, soul, then body, or the other way around?

_____

_____

_____

_____

_____

_____

Affirmations

When we recognize that we need or want to create a shift in ourselves, we need tools and actions to help make it happen. Here is one powerful tool I use.

It takes twenty-one days to establish a new habit, including learning to think differently. Affirmations based on the Word of God are a great way to start re-wiring your brain.

What is an affirmation? It is a statement about you, your life, or your circumstances. You say and think affirmations every day without realizing it or giving it a thought. When you absent-mindedly say/think, "I'm so stupid!", that is an affirmation. When you repeat that affirmation over and over and over for years, it determines what you become. That thought becomes a belief and your mind takes it as truth.

Studies have shown that we think up to approximately 60,000 thoughts a day and about 80% of those are negative. And we repeat those negative thoughts again and again. If you begin speaking all those thoughts out loud so that you hear them and become aware of them, it will shock you how negative it is in your own head. You would never talk to another person that way, so why is it okay to talk to yourself that way?

Bottom line, it's not okay and it does not align with what God says about us either.

The alternative is far more productive and positive. When we intentionally write and speak positive affirmations, we begin to shift the belief system in our heads. Over time, we retrain our brains – we, literally, rewire how our brains think and process information. When we use God's Word as the basis for our affirmations, it begins to get powerful.

I have found for myself that I must speak them out loud to get the most effect from affirmations. There is something that happens when you hear your own voice affirming yourself. It is also great to post a couple on your bathroom mirror, so you see them in the morning. It's really helpful to repeat them out loud multiple times a day, especially when you are first getting started and working on creating the mental shift. It may feel funny at first to say things out loud, but I promise you, it works!

Here is a list of ten affirmations and scriptures to get you started:

1. **I am enough.**

   "I am created in the image of God, the image of perfection."
   Genesis 1:27

"For you created my inmost being; you knit me together in my mother's womb. I praise you because I am fearfully and wonderfully made."

Psalm 139:13

2. I matter.

"For I am God's masterpiece. He has created me anew in Christ Jesus, so I can do all the good things He planned for me long ago."

Ephesians 2:10

3. I am here on purpose for a purpose.

"11 It's in Christ that we find out who we are and what we are living for . . . 12 part of the overall purpose he is working out in everything and everyone."

Ephesians 1:11–12 (MSG)

"You, [God], saw me before I was born and scheduled each day of my life before I began to breathe. Every day was recorded in your book!"

Psalm 139:16 (TLB)

4. I am a daughter of the King!

"But you are God's chosen treasure...a spiritual "nation" set apart as God's devoted ones. He called you out of darkness to experience his marvelous light, and now he claims you as his very own."

1 Peter 2:9 The Passion Translation (TPT)

"See what great love the Father has lavished on us, that we should be called children of God! And that is what we are!"

1 John 3:1

20

5. **God has designed a good life for me; all things are working in my favor.**

"God causes all things to work together for good to those who love God, to those who are called according to His purpose."

Romans 8:28

6. **I have everything I need to live an abundant life.**

"By his divine power, God has given us everything we need for living a godly life. We have received all of this by coming to know him, the one who called us to himself by means of his marvelous glory and excellence."

2 Peter 1:3

7. **I am favored and blessed.**

"For the Lord God is brighter than the brilliance of a sunrise!
Wrapping himself around me like a shield,
he is so generous with his gifts of grace and glory.
Those who walk along his paths with integrity
will never lack one thing they need, for he provides it all!"

Psalm 84:11

8. **I am not a slave to sin; I have been set free.**

"And now you celebrate your freedom from your former master—sin. You've left its bondage, and now God's perfect righteousness holds power over you as his loving servants."

Romans 6:18

9. **I am well able to do all that God has called me to do.**

"Yes, God is more than ready to overwhelm you with every form of grace, so that you will have more than enough of

everything, every moment, and in every way. He will make you overflow with abundance in every good thing you do."

2 Cor. 9:8

10. **I am financially sound and able to give generously.**

    "The Lord is my Shepherd, I lack nothing."

    Psalms 23:1

    "I am convinced that my God will fully satisfy every need you have, for I have seen the abundant riches of glory revealed to me through the Anointed One, Jesus Christ!"

    Philippians 4:19

It is perfectly fine to write your own affirmations as well. If you have a Bible verse that is important to you, make it into an affirmation and run with it.

Below are additional examples of positive, daily affirmations that I use personally. Although not scripturally based, they are in full alignment with how Christ made me.

1. I live daily in agreement with my values and principles.
2. I claim and own my power to do good in the world.
3. I move in excellence, not perfection.
4. I am clear-minded and focused.
5. I live true to my values and do not compromise for anyone.
6. I use my time wisely and effectively.
7. I flow in the Spirit and easily hear His voice.

22

8. I appreciate money and welcome it as it is a symbol of freedom.
9. I open my mind, heart, and spirit to receive abundance.
10. I am wise with money.
11. I am loved and accepted.
12. I expand in abundance, success, and love every day as I inspire those around me to do the same.
13. I am a magnet to abundant and blissful miracles daily.
14. I have all the willpower I need to accomplish my goals.
15. I speak my mind, respectfully but with conviction.

It's fine to start small with one or two affirmations. Pick the one(s) that resonate the most with you, commit to speaking it every day, and then build from there. It may help to associate it with something you do every day like brushing your teeth or combing your hair until it becomes a habit.

Journey Milestones:

1. Write down area(s) of your life that you want to begin using positive statements to make a change. (Some ideas are relationships, self-worth, finances, your future, your purpose, breaking a bad habit, or creating a new habit.)

_____

_____

_____

_____

_____

_____

2. Write one or two affirmations for each of the areas you
   listed in question (Just ensure they include what you DO
   want, not what you don't want, and that it is a positive
   outcome.)

_____

_____

_____

_____

_____

Chapter 2: Who is God, really?

So, who is God really? And Jesus? What about Him? And the Holy Spirit – is He watching and waiting for me to mess up so He can correct me? Read on and see what I think.

God. Father God. Abba.

The Man Upstairs. The Great I AM. Jehovah. Whatever name you call Him or how you think about Him, know that He always has a father's heart towards you. ALWAYS.

When you were a very young child just learning to walk, typically, your parents encouraged you with, "Come to me, baby. You can do this". When you took that first step and then sat down, they were thrilled. Then came more steps and they were just as thrilled! And when you walked from Mom to Dad grinning, they were beaming with joy and pride. This is how God our Father looks at you. Our earthly parents will let us down and many of them fail us big time. This is true around the globe and throughout time. Abba Father, Daddy

God is the example, the standard, the one true God who loves you perfectly, wholly, and completely.

Just as your dad may have done, Father God watches over us when we are awake and when we sleep. He looks at us with love, joy, and pride even when we fail and make mistakes – any mistake. And, just as a good dad will bring correction and education when needed, Father God does the same, but He is always motivated out of love for you and a desire to see you reach your full potential. God will never smack you down to harm you or 'put you in your place'. That is never His heart or motivation.

In my early years as a Christian, this was not the impression I picked up on. There was more teaching of the judgment of God, the wrath of God, and the use of fear as a motivator. As an adult, I know that fear is not ever a good motivator if you want someone to sustain a relationship and change their behavior. Fear is an avoidance mechanism, and it can change behavior for a period of time, but it only changes the outward behavior not the internal motivation of the heart. Only love can do that.

Our Heavenly Father would have you know that you are loved. He loves you deeply, thoroughly, and completely.

Warts and all. Big mistakes, little mistakes, HUMONGOUS mistakes. Not even one of them changes His love for you. We can cause Him to pull back from us and He will not bless our wrong choices – He cannot go against His character and will never change from His Word that He has written. *"God is not a man that He should lie"* (Numbers 23:19) and *"There is no shadow of turning with Him."* (James 1:17). His love is unending, ever hopeful that you will turn your face to Him and lift your arms to Him to be picked up and returned to relationship. One single, simple step from you back toward Him, and He will bridge decades of distance in a heartbeat and embrace you as only He can.

Journey Milestones:

1. Regardless of your dad's approach to raising you, God is a good Father, and He sets the standard of what a Dad is supposed to be. Journal about how you'd like your relationship with your heavenly Father to be.

_____

_____

_____

_____

_____

_____

2. What does it mean to you to accept the Father's love for you? What change can it bring about in you?

_____

_____

_____

_____

_____

Jesus

Jesus. Lord. Savior. Redeemer. Only Son of the Father. King. Warrior. Overcomer. Brother. Friend. Joint-Heir. Died, Risen, Ascended, and Coming Again.

Remember the song, "What a Friend we have in Jesus"? (Joseph Scriven, mid-1800's). Here are some of the words,

What a friend we have in Jesus
All our sins and griefs to bear
What a privilege to carry
Everything to God in prayer.

Oh, what peace we often forfeit
Oh, what needless pain we bear
All because we do not carry
Everything to God in prayer.

Jesus. One of the most controversial names in history. Some
people use his name as a swear word. Some think he is *a* son
of God. Christians believe He is *the* Son of God. When he
was alive, he threatened the religious institutions of his day
with His claims and new way of thinking and being. He was
highly unusual. Many didn't know what to make of Him. It
was obvious to many that He heard from God – maybe a
prophet? An anointed teacher? To the 12 men who became
His disciples, he was revelatory! How could someone who
was just a man know the things Jesus knew? Jesus had a
sense of humor and an easy style and yet an intensity they had
never experienced before. He thought differently than
anyone they had ever encountered. Once the miracles
started, even the disciples were in awe and stunned at what
He was able to do.

From our perspective of looking back on history, it is somewhat commonplace and well known of how Jesus did miraculous things. We just know them. They are a given. For the people who were alive with Jesus, it was unheard of and unimaginable. Never in their wildest imaginations could they have conceived of changing water into wine or feeding five thousand people with 5 small loaves of bread and three fish. There was no template or precedent or even an ability to expect that being feasible.

Fast forward to our day and time. We have so much history to look back on and to see how Jesus has been portrayed, understood and misunderstood for two centuries. Is He still relevant in the 21st century? What role does He want to play in my life and what role do I want Him to play? Can I trust Him with my deepest secret longings, with my doubts and fears and of course, can He overlook all the mistakes I've made? I will attempt to answer these types of questions based on the 50+ years that I have been in a relationship with Him and my experiences. I don't want this to be too heavy or "religious sounding" but we need a foundation to build on and that is my intention in the rest of this chapter. Let's start with the ending of Jesus life on earth – His death on the cross.

Why was the cross necessary?

Jesus' first priority is to have a great relationship with us. It brings Him joy and the utmost satisfaction when we are close to Him. He has ideas to share with us, jokes to tell us, wisdom to share, perspectives that will raise us up to higher levels. All good stuff! What keeps us from being in that space? Our choices usually. Our wrong behaviors, actions and thoughts puts a barrier between us and God. If I'm not sure I trust you or I'm not sure I believe in you, it's hard to have a solid relationship. If you're a mom, its similar to when kids misbehave – you still love them, but you don't tolerate bad behavior. Jesus has the same principle but on a much larger scale and with more severe consequences. Without Jesus dying on the cross, we would have eternal separation from God – which is exactly what hell is. Also, without the cross, we would still be under the Law of Moses (think Old Testament) instead of being under grace (God's favor).

Jesus allowed himself to be crucified to fulfill, once-and-for-all, the Old Testament requirement of the giving of life to account for sin. It can be hard to understand this approach since we are so far removed from anything even close to this. Jesus had to live a life without sin so He could symbolically take on the sin of all people throughout history and become the final sacrifice. It is through what Jesus accomplished on the cross that we have a relationship with The Father, Jesus, and the Holy Spirit. The blood of Jesus that fell to the earth while He was on the cross redeemed the physical earth and all of humankind. I have not been to Israel yet, but I will go to Golgotha and experience where our salvation occurred so many years ago. Israel is where Jesus lived and walked, and I want to see it for myself.

Beyond giving His life to redeem us, Jesus is SO much more. He has been described as The Way, The Truth, and The Life and that is exactly what He is. Let's go deeper into exactly what that means.

Jesus is THE WAY.

"One-way God said to get to heaven, Jesus is the only way" (Child Evangelism Fellowship song). These are words from a song I learned as a child and they have been my truth my entire life. Jesus is my solid rock, my foundation, my bottom line. When life's storms have hit – and they have been many and varied, I go to another song, "On Christ the Solid Rock I Stand (Edward Mote, 1834)". A more recent song that is my go-to is In Christ Alone by Keith and Kristyn Getty, 2001. This is my Jesus. The Lord I worship. The King I serve. My one and only Redeemer. Jesus, He who gave His life willingly for me on the cross, the worst form of punishment and pain I can conceive of. This is Jesus who calls me by name with a depth of love that only His suffering can bring. Him whom I love with all of my heart and in every possible way I know how to love. He is my example of how to be, how to live, how to build relationships, what to be willing to die for, and everything in-between.

Jesus is TRUTH.

Have you ever wondered if Jesus had opinions? My opinions are how I think about and perceive things. They may or may not be true, but it is my perspective. I perceive that from his earliest ages, He was in relationship with the Father and only formed his perspectives and opinions on the written and spoken word of God. Having an opinion is not a sin. If we act on our opinions and our actions or if our heart motive does not align with God's Word, then we can move into sin. In the Bible, we are told and shown that Jesus never sinned – not even once, which tells me He also had the right heart motives.

I have always been a truth seeker from as far back as I can remember. I love TRUTH even when it is hard to take. I don't want surface or shallow half-truths. Give me the real thing every time. I need to know the real deal – the bottom-line truth. This is what Jesus taught, lived, and represents in every facet of His life and being.

Jesus is LIGHT

Another aspect of Jesus is that He is Light. In Him, there is no darkness in any way, shape, or form. Nor was there ever. You cannot fake light. There may be 'artificial' light that is not the sun, but even that light is still…light. On earth, we do not know or possess anything that is 100% pure. Even the purest gold or silver still has slight imperfections. Jesus did not have a single, slight imperfection. He was 100% God and 100% human simultaneously.

When we come to Jesus and ask Him into our lives, He shines His light in our hearts – that inner being where the real 'me' exists – my mind, will, and emotions. Because of the cross, He is able to wash away our deep hurts, fears, wrongdoings, wrong thinking, wrong heart motivations, and all the other things that don't align with TRUTH.

It is a lifelong process that we will not totally complete this side of heaven but in that initial instant that He enters our life, ALL is changed. We miraculously go from being on the wrong side of the door to being on the right side. He moves us, we don't move ourselves. We instantly morph from being an enemy of God in a spiritual sense to being redeemed back into full relationship with Him. The Bible calls this repentance – changing our thinking and allowing Jesus and the Holy Spirit to begin growing us into His image.

Jesus is LIFE

For me, the opposite of life was not death, it was just existing. There were years when I went through the motions of living but there was no spark of life. I was unmotivated, depressed, and weighed down with guilt and shame. I gained weight, cried myself to sleep at night, wished things were different – but did nothing about it. I only wore blah-colored clothes, so I didn't stand out or get seen. I felt transparent and I wanted to remain that way. I felt like a victim to my circumstances and powerless to do anything about it. I was still going to church regularly, had a good job, was married, had a nice house – from the outside it should have all been fine. But it wasn't.

Jesus said, "*I came to bring life and life abundantly*" (John 10:10). I knew the scripture well, had quoted it frequently, but it sure seemed like it must apply to everyone else but me. Where were my dreams? Where was the joy I used to have? Where did my happiness go? I would never do anything to harm myself but there were times I sure prayed for God to take me home. It was like, "Either we need to do something different, or You need to bring me home to heaven."

Jesus brought me back to LIFE. It was not like switching the light on – it took time; there was a stirring in my heart, a flutter of new life like a butterfly. He brought the right people into my circle, He brought the right teachings I needed to hear, He opened my spiritual ears to hear Him again. Life returned and the joy came back and the light in my eyes sparkled again. Life absolutely still had challenges. The outward circumstances had not changed yet He brought life within me. I had given up hope of a better way and He restored my hope.

When I say Jesus is life, there are multiple facets, too. He gave me life back in the form of hope and sparkle. Jesus also gave us eternal life with Him through the cross. Yes, it all comes back to the cross. Jesus conquered sin, death, hell, and the grave when He died as our sacrificial lamb.

In Jewish tradition, once a year a family would all lay their hands on a lamb with the symbolism of transferring their failures and sins onto that lamb. The father would then take that sacrificial lamb to the temple to the priests and the death of that lamb, and the shedding of its blood cleansed that family for another year, but this same ritual had to be continuously repeated annually or the family was out of relationship with God and would not be blessed. *"Without the shedding of blood, there is no remission for sin"* (Heb 9:22). Jesus died on the cross once-and-for-all as the spotless, sinless Lamb of God for all of mankind. In one selfless act of love, Jesus created a way for every single human being from Adam to the very last person who will ever be born prior to the end of the world to be restored to right relationship with God.

Because the blood of Jesus was shed on the cross, God the Father eternally sees you as His redeemed child. This is why and how the Father always looks at us with loving eyes. It is also why He so badly desires us and draws us into a relationship with Himself, Jesus, and the Holy Spirit. Without the blood of Jesus in our lives, covering our wrongs, we are separated from God and He has to look at us differently. This is also why it is so black and white – either you are covered by the blood of Jesus or you are not. There is no 'maybe'.

Enter unconditional love. When we say God loves us unconditionally, we mean just that. God does not have the attitude or perspective of "If you do this for Me, then I will love you or love you more". That is a human construct and a condition of love. (There are IF – THEN situations in the Word of God, but they don't apply here). We are human – designed to be human by God and He knows we are going to make mistakes every day. But - the BEST NEWS EVER – He already accounted for that when He made us! He is not ever surprised that we fall or fail.

As God, He knows there is nothing we can do to save ourselves. And that's perfectly OK with Him. He's got it covered! Before Jesus died on the cross, the Jewish nation – God's chosen people, used the God-given sacrifice of animals to remove their sin by the shedding of blood. When Jesus was alive, the need for sacrifice continued and it was still limited to Jews.

The very moment Jesus died, there was an earthquake and the curtain in the Jewish temple in Jerusalem was ripped from top to bottom. The significance of this is life-changing for every person born from that moment on. God provided Jesus as the final sacrificial lamb and extended salvation not only to the Jewish nation but to non-Jews as well. This is you and me (the non-Jews).

God's Word uses the description of grafting a branch onto a tree to illustrate this process. The trunk of the tree and the existing branches remain in place but by making a cut in the bark of a tree, you can graft a branch from a different kind of tree and the two grow together. The main branch of the tree provides nutrients and water from the roots just like the original branches. As non-Jews, we enjoy all the benefits of the roots and the original tree just as if we had always been a part of it.

This is how God has already provided for us. We call this grace, and it is God's unconditional love that He includes ALL of us under the blood of Jesus.

Journey Milestones:

1. Jesus is the Way, the Truth, and the Life. Which description of Jesus did you most relate to and why?

   _____

   _____

   _____

   _____

   _____

   _____

2. Which description of Jesus do you need more of and why? Begin to thank Him now for coming in the way you need Him.

   _____

   _____

   _____

   _____

   _____

   _____

The Holy Spirit

When Jesus was alive and on earth, He was human and could only be in one place at a time, just like us. When He ascended to heaven, God gave us a new gift in the third person of the Trinity – the Holy Spirit. In the original Greek, the Holy Spirit is described as the "Paraclete" – the Comforter. He is God's gift to each of us and the Holy Spirit can be everywhere all the time! The Holy Spirit is our teacher, guide, inner small voice, cheerleader, coach, corrections officer, and, most importantly, our best friend.

When we ask Jesus to come into our lives, we automatically get the best package deal in all of eternity. The Holy Spirit enters our hearts and our lives and is with us forever. When you have that nudge in a direction to go or you hear that voice in your ear bringing truth and guidance, that is the Holy Spirit. When you feel that check or restriction or warning of danger – that, too, is the Holy Spirit. When you have a feeling like a hunger pain in your stomach, but you know it's not that you need food, that also is the Holy Spirit. When you can look at another person and see the Light of Christ in them, it is the Holy Spirit in you showing you the Holy Spirit in them. Every follower of Jesus around the world today has the Holy

Spirit. That is why you can travel anywhere on earth and connect instantly with other Christians. He is our commonality across languages, cultures, races, or views. The Holy Spirit is constantly drawing us upwards, toward the Father, towards our higher purpose. As we grow in the Holy Spirit and learn to follow His voice, we move into the Flow of Heaven and we encounter His blessings and His truth.

When we first come to Christ, we have a lot of internal baggage, hurts, wounds, rejection, self-judgments, fears, etc. These can limit the room we have in our hearts for the Holy Spirit. Over time, as we are willing, He will show us how to clean spiritual house and make more room for Him to work and flow in and through us.

We may also have hardness in our hearts from the way we've been treated and from the circumstances we have lived through. The Holy Spirit will also help us to soften our hearts and learn to trust Him and other people again. We reject others when we feel rejected. This can also cause us to reject God in all forms.

The Holy Spirit will bring us into His unconditional love and give us a view of how He sees us. What He sees is the person God always intended you to be – how He perfectly designed you in His image with gifts, talents, and abilities that were always intended for good. THIS is the real you. When you peel back all the layers of gunk that have accumulated on you over time, the person you ARE is still there. God has never lost sight of YOU even when you have. What He designed and intended is good and that is how He looks at you. The load of sin, shame, guilt, condemnation, judgment, physical scars, mental scars, emotional scars, spiritual scars, mistakes, wrong choices, hate, fear, divorce, murder, and every other thing you can name or associate with yourself do not define you to God. He does not label us 'good' or 'bad'. What He made is always good; He sees us under the blood of Jesus or not (yet). When we are under the blood of Jesus – when we have asked Jesus into our lives and had Him wash away our sin – God sees YOU. The YOU He spoke into being. The YOU He created with love, true love, and nothing but love. We recall our mistakes, and we force ourselves to live with them, but God does not. This is not to say that God removes the consequences of our choices; we still have to live with the results and outcomes. However, God moves into those consequences with us and brings grace and redemption and will use them for our good instead of continuing harm.

If you have read this far and don't have Jesus in your life, let's change that right now. It is so simple – don't try to make it hard. Say the following prayer and mean it:

Jesus, I have made a mess of my life and I'm ready to do something about it. I ask You to come and be part of my life. I know I've made a LOT of mistakes and I am sorry for them. Please forgive me, make my heart clean, and let's be friends from this moment on. I believe you are God's son and that You died on the cross so I can be part of Your family. Change me from the inside out and give me a desire to grow closer to You. Please send me the Holy Spirit too, so I have Him with me all the time. Thank you for your love and forgiveness. Amen. (So, let it be!)

When you ask Jesus to come and be part of your life, angels in heaven rejoice and ring a bell! This is the BEST choice you will ever make for life here on earth and for eternity. Welcome to the family!

Journey Milestone:

1. How will you plan to listen more to and for the Holy Spirit? By journaling with Him? Spending time in meditation listening for Him to speak to you? Simply talking to Him throughout your day? Write down and commit to your approach.

_____

_____

_____

_____

_____

_____

Part 2: Becoming Myself

Chapters 3 – 12 are all about the journey of becoming the real you – the you God designed you to be. Much of finding who you are is letting go of who you are not and stepping away from other people's opinions of who you 'should' be. You are YOU. Perfectly imperfect you. You are unique, one-of-a-kind in all of history, and you matter!

One of the quotes I use is from the Chesire Cat in Alice in Wonderland, "When you don't know where you are going, any road will get you there." Becoming yourself involves engaging with your life's purpose and being intentional about your journey. This entire section of the book will walk you through uncovering what is already inside you – placed there by God. It also encourages you to let go of the baggage that slows you down.

God is with you every step of the way and He will provide all you need to get where you need to go. Being in a partnership with Him is much easier than going it alone. He leads us in kindness and gives us good gifts along the way. Hard times do and will happen – it's a given in life. The weight and burdens are so much easier to carry when God is picking up the majority of the lift.

Chapter 3: The Destination

"If you don't know where you're going, any road will get you there."

Cheshire Cat, Alice in Wonderland

I want to introduce a Bible character and story to illustrate someone whose life plan didn't follow a straight line but was still divinely orchestrated. Joseph was the 11th son of Jacob and Jacob was a grandson of Abraham, one of the founding fathers of the Old Testament of the Bible. Joseph's story is recorded in Genesis 39. Let's start with Genesis 39:11:

> *11 When Joseph was taken to Egypt by the Ishmaelite traders....*

Spoiler alert - we start out knowing the end of the story – that Joseph becomes the second-most important man in Egypt behind Pharaoh and saves the entire nation from famine, but let's back up and look at Joseph's journey from somewhere in the middle.

Joseph had grown up the much-beloved, favorite son of his

father Jacob. Jacob had a "coat of many colors" made specifically for Joseph and Joseph repeatedly had dreams where he saw his brothers becoming subordinate to him or lower than him. His older brothers didn't like him and were, in fact, jealous and despised him. Additionally, Joseph's dreams continued to point out how different he was from the rest of them. Benjamin was the only son with the same mother which also added to the relationship challenges. Perhaps blended families weren't easy then either. Joseph's brothers plotted to get rid of him, threw him in a well or a pit, and ultimately sold him to a slave trader.

Let's look at the scripture word by word:

"*When*" – Not 'if', not 'sort of' – 'when'. It was a historical fact. It happened.

"*Was taken*" — Against his will and not to any place he would have ever chosen to go out of his own volition. Egypt was beyond the border or boundary of where Joseph or Jacob would've expected to travel in their lifetime.

"*By Ishmaelite traders*" – These men were wandering traders who made their livelihood by selling animals and people as slaves. I imagine them as not very educated or considerate. The Ishmaelite men were also known as Midianites which translates into "A Place of Judgment."

Is there a plan for me?

How many of us have experienced a situation where we could say we were in a pit? Be it a pit of despair, a pit of our digging, or someone else's digging, or life taking a downward turn?

Joseph was thrown into a pit or a well by his brothers. The symbolism here is planned by God. An empty 'well' in our own lives can easily become a pit of distraction or hopelessness for each of us. (This is why it is so important to keep our 'spiritual wells' full and flowing with fresh clean, holy water. This happens through praise and worship and soaking in the Word of God.)

Joseph so easily could've been bitter and angry but the Bible never even hints that he allowed self-pity or concern to afflict him. Joseph had to be a man of integrity and faith. His journey certainly took some odd twists and turns out of the ordinary. Most anyone would look at what happened and see a journey interrupted. This bright, intelligent, gifted young man with incredible talent was being "wasted" as a slave. What would have appeared to be a significant detour in his journey to becoming was a training and proving ground for the profound plan that God had in place all the while. As you read to the end of Joseph's story, he is empowered by God to interpret Pharaoh's awful dreams which indicate severe famine is coming to Egypt. Joseph spends the next 7 years leading the nation-wide effort of storing food and making preparations. As the 7 years of famine occur, Joseph's brothers come to Egypt in search of food and the brothers are reunited through extreme grace shown by Joseph. Their father Jacob is also able to see his missing son before Jacobs passes on. As mentioned above, the entire story is found in Genesis 39.

What bothers you the most about *your* journey? Is it the hardships, the seeming insignificance of where you are and what you're doing, the mistakes you've made, the attacks others have made on you or your dreams? Each of us will have our experiences and circumstances in life. We can either choose to trust that we are right on track or we can allow negativity to rob us of important lessons that contribute to the total picture of who we are becoming in Jesus.

We will talk more about how wrong choices can affect our destiny but don't be afraid to live and make decisions to move forward with your life. Talking to God daily helps a lot. If you don't have a daily walk with Jesus, now is the right time to start. Pray the following:

> *Lord, I do want to have a stronger relationship with You, and I would like to have your input on my decisions, my destinations, and every other aspect of my life. I ask for you to bring Your Light into my life. I want to live a life of significance. Please come and show me Your ways. Amen. (So, let it be!)*

Just as Joseph went willingly into the life God had planned for him though it wasn't what he planned for himself, we each get to choose to be God's partner in life or we can choose to do it ourselves. If you are fighting God on a decision, you probably don't want to win. I have argued with God many times on many subjects and seriously questioned His timing, reasoning, and motivation. What I learned the hard way is, God always has a good reason for His leading and if I will trust Him, it turns out better than I expected.

God DOES have a plan for your life. Jeremiah 29:11 says it this way:

> *"For I know the plans I have for you, plans to give you a hope*

and a future."

God will use every decision we've ever made, every experience, all of our circumstances to grow us into the person He designed us to be.

When a caterpillar is in the process of becoming a butterfly there is a significant struggle involved to emerge from the cocoon. That struggle forces extra fluid out of the body and allows the wings to complete development. Without the struggle, the butterfly would never be able to get off the ground.

God can take our "mess" and turn it into our "message". We often get tripped up in life in the very areas that we are most gifted. While God has a plan for good, there is the enemy of our lives who will take us off track every chance he gets.

Journey Milestones:

1. If you prayed the prayer in this chapter, note it here with the date and what your experience was as you asked Jesus into your life.

   _____

   _____

_____

_____

_____

_____

2. Record your thoughts and questions that popped up as you read this section. Come back to this later and ask the Holy Spirit to bring you answers.

_____

_____

_____

_____

_____

How do I get back if I'm off track?

First off, we ALL get off track at different points in our lives. Don't let your mind, your ego, or the enemy of your soul tell you differently. Satan likes nothing better than to tell you how awful you are – beyond hope – there is no way back. It's a lie from the pit of hell! Do NOT buy into it.

Regardless of what you've done, where you are right now, how 'bad' you think you are, or even how bad you are, God wants nothing more than to reconnect with you. When you turn your face towards God, He is instantly aware of and ready for you. If you will take one step towards Him, He will bridge the gap for whatever distance is between you. It takes being honest with yourself and Him. Own up to your mistakes – do not blame anyone else or circumstances or your mom. It's you. Own it. Then ask Him to come and, as sure as the sun will come up tomorrow, He will be there. God is a fair and just God. He will not save us from the consequences of our choices, but He will save us, and He will walk with you every step of the way and redeem it all.

Be aware, God will not be manipulated. If you are used to getting your way through whatever means, it will not work with Him. He sees and judges the intentions of the heart. You have to be brutally honest first with yourself and also with God. He knows it all anyway. You cannot, cannot hide anything from Him, so why try?

The Bible talks about manipulation being a type of witchcraft.

It is not OK and must be stopped and repented of. (Remember, repent means 'to think again – to think differently'.) If you have learned to manipulate people or the system, it is a habit that has to be broken and changed. Again, ask God for the help you need to change your behavior. It may feel awkward at first to not manipulate and control, but it is a non-negotiable with Him. Let your YES be YES and your NO be NO. Speak your truth and mean it. Do not sugar coat things to get your way. Do not twist the truth even a little to make things look better. A rock is not a 'natural paper weight' – it's a rock. Don't dress it up to appear to be more than it is.

Here is a prayer to get back into relationship with the Father, Jesus, and the Holy Spirit. This can be prayed any time, day or night when you want to reconnect.

> *Father, I know that You are immovable; it is me that has moved and drifted away from where You want me to be. I am sincerely sorry for the wrong things I've done and for how far away from you I've let myself go. Please forgive me for the wrong things I've done, the wrong attitudes I have, and the stubbornness and shame that keeps me from turning back to You. Lord, I need you in my life and I ask right now to*

reconnect with You. Please make my heart clean again and draw me back to You. I don't want to do life alone anymore. I am willing to give up my agenda and my plan for yours because I know Yours is always better. Please meet me here, right now, and fill me with Your Holy Spirit. I need Your peace and your assurance. Thank you, God. Amen.

Your next step is to find another believer and tell them you have reconnected with God. You need to speak it out loud to another person, for accountability, but also to remind yourself it is real. Satan will try to steal this away, convince you it didn't happen, and that you are too far gone. Don't listen to him. You are precious in God's eyes – so important that He sent Jesus to die on the cross for you.

I also encourage you to begin thanking God for His mercy and for where He has worked in your life even when you haven't seen it or been aware. The 'attitude of gratitude' is key to remaining in a relationship with our Heavenly Father and Jesus. They have given us the opportunity for life AND eternal life. What's not to be grateful for? Thank God and praise Him for who He is and His holiness and righteousness. God has nothing but good thoughts about and for you. We, again, quote Jeremiah 29:11:

"For I know the plans I have for you says the Lord; plans to do you good and not to harm you, plans to give you a HOPE and a FUTURE."

As we are grateful to God and express that to Him, He can move even more in us and on our behalf. I have to repeat, God loves you SO MUCH He sent His son to die! God wrote out all the days of your life before He even created the earth. He's just that amazing! God accounted for our humanness and our faults and our sin when He created man. It's OK to be human – we are made in His image and He calls us GOOD! It is we who talk down about ourselves and think less of ourselves than God does. It is not a sin to be human! We get to spend our lives becoming more like Jesus, but in His plan, He already accounted for our stupidity, our stubbornness, and our susceptibility to sin. He's got it covered. (This is not a license to go be more stupid, however.) I will also mention that if you think your sin is too great for God to account for or forgive, that is a form of pride and needs to be dealt with. NO ONE is beyond the blood of Jesus and the work of the cross. If this sounds familiar to you, ask God to help you overcome that attitude of pride.

Journey Milestones:

1. What areas of your life do you recognize are off track and you want to change?

_____

_____

_____

_____

_____

2. It is through action and commitment that our shifts come. Record action steps you will take to start getting back on track. Don't be afraid to start small and simple - even the smallest step forward is progress. your life.

_____

_____

_____

_____

_____

_____

58

How do I keep growing?

Joseph's keys to growth were:

1. He maintained a good attitude regardless of his circumstances
2. He stayed true to himself
3. He used his natural skills to serve right where he was
4. Joseph remained humble while at the top just as he was at the bottom

Let's look at these in more depth.

1. Joseph maintained a good attitude regardless. As we've already discussed, not once does scripture record Joseph grumbling or complaining. Not when he was in the pit of the well, sold into slavery, in prison, or when he was serving kings and managers. Joseph trusted that God had a plan to get him out of his present difficulties. God understands and has compassion for us struggling, questioning, or doubting. God does not tolerate us having unbelief. When we grumble, complain, and mutter under our breath about how bad we have it in life, we are exhibiting unbelief. This same grumbling and unbelief are what kept the people of Israel in the desert for forty years.

The antidote to unbelief is gratitude and praise for God.

When my eyes are on His glory and I stop and recount all the marvelous things God has done for me, it will hush the critic that wants to complain so loudly. Your eyes can only look in one place at a time; choose wisely where you have your focus. If I am looking at my empty bank account or wondering why my boss hates me so much or why it's raining yet again today, it's hard to be in gratitude and gratefulness. God's Word says He will provide and that His arm is never short. When your eyes, both spiritual and natural, are focused on the Lord and His purposes on the earth and for other people, you come into a rhythm with the Holy Spirit that keeps you moving forward and helps you cooperate with what God is already doing in your life and those around you and your blessings will be multiplied.

When my family and I were going through a really tough time in our lives, I asked God how I should be praying. He taught me a principle that I have lived by ever since. When you are in great need, pray for others. It's fine to pray for yourself too but keep your focus on others. When you do this, God will appoint intercessors and pray-ers around the world to be praying for you and your need. We often don't know exactly how to pray for ourselves objectively. I find it easier to pray for others and hear from the Lord on what to pray for them than for myself. I have my own agenda in my heart and mind when I pray for my needs; I have God's objectives in mind more often when I pray for others.

2. He stayed true to himself. Joseph didn't compromise who he was or what he believed in to please those around him or to accommodate where he was in life. It was this integrity and putting his natural skills to use for Gods' glory that brought him favor and recognition.

The Bible tells us that your gifts will promote you. You don't have to sell yourself or what you're capable of. When you have God's favor, you will be noticed. So, you ask, "How do I get God's favor?" It comes from relationship and being in His Presence, reading His Word, and inviting Him into your everyday life and circumstance. It comes from being obedient to His Word and the promptings of the Holy Spirit. As you develop that relationship with Him, you hear His voice more quickly and you recognize the little promptings, those nudges that encourage you to talk to someone, give that person money, pray for that person over there, or pick up the phone and call someone and she's responded that your call was so needed, and at the right time. It is a progression over a lifetime of being in a relationship with your Heavenly Father, the Lord Jesus, and the Holy Spirit.

Joseph knew who he was, and he knew that God Almighty was on his side and was his true source of life. If you cannot say that God is your true source of life, pray this prayer with me:

> *Father, I recognize my need and my desire for more of You in my life. I do want to live true to who You made me to be, without compromise. I ask that You wash away the dust and dirt of the past and make me clean and refreshed so that going forward I can easily hear Your voice and know what is best for me and how I can serve You more. Like Joseph, let me not complain about what I experience; instead, help me to see how You are moving or want to move in my circumstances to make me a blessing to those around me and also to bring more blessing into my life. I choose to honor You with all I say and do, and I thank You for making me exactly who I am. Thank you for loving me in spite of all my slip-ups. I love you, Lord. Amen.*

3. Joseph used his natural skills to serve right where he was. It's easy to project into the future (even though we have no clue what that future will bring) and think, "If I get that other job, it will be so much better, and I will be so much happier". "When I change jobs and have a different manager, they will see how good of a worker I am and not be on my case all the time, micro-managing me."

I can use my imagination and think that Joseph probably had dreams of a different or better future. If he did, it didn't get in the way of him applying himself right where he was. He also found ways to use his God-given talents, abilities, and gifts everywhere he was. Joseph had to be gifted at building relationships which meant he cared about other people, talked to them, and found a significant way to help them. If he had remained quiet, sullen, and grumbling, he would not have been noticed and acknowledged, and eventually promoted as he was. Joseph gave his work all the quality he could at the time. He did his best in every circumstance by simply being himself and using his skill sets. I also have to believe that living in a stinking, rotten prison did not give him the best opportunity to use his leadership skills; but he found a way to be useful, nonetheless. That is also a demonstration of humility.

4. Joseph remained humble while at the top (second in command of the country) just as he was at the bottom (serving while in prison). Being humble does not mean being a doormat. True humility is when I know my worth and my value and from that place of confidence, I choose to put others' needs before my own. It also involves the awareness that all that I have has been given to me as a gift and it can be gone tomorrow. If and when I think that I am in control and I'm the most important person whose needs must be met, I set myself up for a fall. Joseph put out the same quality and amount of effort when he was serving in the lowest position as a slave that he did when he was second in command of an entire nation. Personal integrity and a selfless motivation to do not only what is right but of the greatest service will get you noticed, bring you favor, and see you succeed in all you do.

When you add reliance on God for your guidance, strength, and provision, wanting to do His will and bring Him glory in what you achieve, you have a formula for ongoing, positive success. When you are serving God in the position you are called to, there is no trivial or meaningless job or task. It is doing ALL things with a desire to bring God the glory.

This is what Joseph did regardless of where he was, and it is why he was able to do it with a good attitude and no complaining. He believed that what he was doing brought honor to God as he did it out of obedience and right heart motive. When Joseph was summoned to the King to interpret his awful dreams, Joseph remained true to himself and spoke what the Lord gave him, not watering it down out of fear or enhancing it to make it sound better. He spoke the truth. This also shows humility from Joseph as he knew he had nothing to add to what God had said. He was a mouthpiece to deliver a perfectly worded, heavenly message.

Pride would say, "I can make it better". Humility says, "I will faithfully deliver the word of God exactly as He spoke it". It is easy for us in our thinking to want to 'help' God with His words. I am pretty certain God has a thorough command of languages – ALL of them – and is quite able to state His case without my interpretation.

Journey Milestones:

1. What are your natural skills and abilities that you know are God-designed in you? Everyone has them – do not let yourself off the hook on this question. You DO have natural talents that God will use. I encourage you to write down at least three.

    _____

    _____

    _____

    _____

    _____

    _____

2. How has your attitude been in life? Do you grumble and complain? Do you look for the silver lining in the cloud? Write down what your past attitude has been and then, in the next question, record what you want the future to look like in your life.

_____

_____

_____

_____

_____

_____

3. Write down what you want the future to look like as far
   as your attitude and approach to using your natural talents
   to create a better future.

_____

_____

_____

_____

_____

Chapter 4: Destiny

If you read further in Genesis 39, you'll see that Joseph is bought by Potiphar, the Captain of the Guard for Pharaoh. Potiphar was a seasoned warrior, used to being in command, used to living the good life. Potiphar recognized the talent in Joseph and the Bible tells us that he also knew that Joseph was blessed by God and that God prospered all that Joseph did. This tells us that Potiphar had discernment and was not offended by God. Potiphar gave Joseph more and more responsibility and they were both successful in all they did. Then Potiphar's wife got bored or jealous or just lustful. Joseph refused to compromise his standards and did his best to avoid conflict, but trouble found him yet again. The wife wrongly accused Joseph of attacking her and Joseph once again found himself in a prison.

The prison that Joseph was thrown into was below Potiphar's house. This was a typical building approach used at this time. Joseph once again proved himself a worthy organizer and leader and he was given control of the prison. When

Pharaoh's cupbearer and baker were also placed in jail, Joseph attended to them. I'm sure it was a stinky, revolting place. Joseph correctly interpreted their dreams and, eventually, the cupbearer remembered to tell Pharaoh when he had dreams, and no one could interpret them. Joseph transitions from running Potiphar's house to running the prison for Potiphar to being summoned by Pharaoh – quite a dramatic transition. Keep in mind that years have passed here. Again, the Bible does not hint at a bad attitude, complaint, or depression, but of giving of his whole self to serve the Lord regardless of his circumstances. What tremendous faith!

"When life gives you lemons, make lemonade." This phrase was popular a few years ago but reflects Joseph's Godly attitude. Even the richest man in the kingdom had disturbing dreams that interrupted his sleep and peace of mind. He knew they had significance; he didn't know what it was until Joseph was placed in front of him by the Lord to fulfill his destiny. All those harsh years of preparation and waiting and trial would be overcome and put to good use as the due time in history came for Joseph to step into the next phase of his journey, his destiny, and become the second most important man in his era.

What am I here to accomplish?

I don't expect that many of us will be put in charge of saving
an entire nation from famine. The purpose here is to look at
your destiny as being just as significant in our day as Joseph's
was in his. If you are following the journey that God has
prescribed for you, you're in an important place. It sounds
trite to say that you are the only you, but it is so true. No one
else has the life experience that you've had to put you right in
the place where you are, with the knowledge you have, or to
speak to the exact people that you come in contact with.

When I was growing up, I had a poster in my room for
several years. It was a solitary large tree, beautifully draped
with snow on each branch and in a snow-covered setting.
The inscription on the poster read,

> *"Do not pray for an easy life,*
> *pray to be a strong person".*

I did pray that prayer. I didn't understand in my youth what
it would take to become strong and how hard it could be.
Today I appreciate my strength and I've seen that God has
always been faithful to provide and strengthen me in times of
need.

As I sit here in my current circumstances, I could never have imagined myself being where I am – not at all. I know and understand that I would not have learned to lean on Jesus and would not be the person that I am without difficulties. I am grateful for all I've learned and the spiritual muscle I've built through the many challenges life has brought. But still, I occasionally wish there was a different way to have learned the lessons.

In one of the more difficult times, the Lord showed me that my tears during prayer were being collected in a bottle and that one particular man who was involved in our situation would be impacted for eternity by those tears. The Lord will redeem and use for his glory every situation, every tear, every prayer, and every circumstance. He is a God of creativity even in the midst of trauma. He can be trusted. His grace extends so far to cover us.

During one period in the same difficult situation, I kept using the phrase, "Lord, I'm placing all my eggs in your basket." It was a time that needed immense trust in Jesus beyond anything I've ever been tested in before. At the end of that time, a good friend was praying over me and my husband and used that exact same phrase – which he has probably never uttered since that day! And God was faithful to protect all my 'eggs' that I entrusted to him. I held nothing back because I knew I could not protect even a single egg by myself. It was beyond my control in just about every way. Those eggs represented my five-year-old daughter, my marriage, our provision for food and housing, our future jobs, and our very well being. At one time, we had $12 left to live on. We made it.

Journey Milestone:

1. You are here on purpose and for a purpose. Write down what you know of that purpose including any new impressions you have while reading this book.

_____

_____

_____

_____

_____

_____

Gifts, Talents, and Abilities

I have felt since I was 14 that someday I would go to Africa to minister. It has yet to happen, but I am as hopeful about it today as I've ever been. I don't know how or when, but I believe it will come. As I go through my tough times and days, I can't help but wonder what skill or lesson I am learning that is going to be helpful when I go there.

While I see God's hand in many things I experience, there are other times when I wonder if God is even aware they are happening to me. How could He possibly allow them and never could he, *gasp*, orchestrate them – not for <u>my</u> good! It may not be for my good…but it is for the good of the Kingdom and what He wants for me to learn. My conclusion is that my assessment of the skills I need to go minister in Africa or anywhere is different from what God knows I will need.

Where are you in your Journey? Are you with jealous siblings? In a pit? Learning leadership in a difficult office situation? Learning to deal with death and tragedy? Running a food bank? Simply teaching the Twos and Threes in Sunday school. All of these and every other place we, as women, reside become the training grounds that God uses to hone our skills and prepare us for what comes next and then, after that.

All is Well

Perhaps you are a woman who knows and understands her destiny. You have trusted God that you are on the right track and in the right place at the right time. You don't have a lot of challenges right now.

Are you thinking, *"Is something wrong?"* No! If we were all in the depths of training at the same time, who would be the encouragers? If you are in a settled season of life, part of your job is to look for and look out for the women who are in training and support them. Please don't ever judge another because she's in class and you are not. It is often God's doing and God's timing to allow her to face situations and circumstances for her to learn and grow. And even if she made some questionable choices and got herself in a pickle, don't you dare judge her then either. All you are doing is opening the door for criticism to fall on yourself and God's favor to depart from you.

Journey Milestones:

1. Record things you <u>*know*</u> you are supposed to do in life regardless if you have done them or not, whether you know when and even if you don't have a clue how they can happen.

   _____

   _____

   _____

   _____

   _____

2. Part of stepping into an Unshakeable Life is being brutally honest with yourself about what you're good at and what you know deep inside you are made to do. Digging deep, what does your spirit, the Holy Spirit, and your intuition – that inner knowing – tell you about your purpose?

   _____

   _____

   _____

   _____

Chapter 5: Obstacles

The cross of Jesus split time. When Jesus died, the curtain that was in the Jewish temple in Jerusalem was torn in two, representing that all of us could come to God individually, not just the Jewish priests.

In our individual lives, the cross also splits time. There is life before Jesus and life after Jesus. It only takes a moment for that curtain in our lives to rip right down the middle and a lifetime to fully comprehend what it means. It is because of the cross that any person will ever enter into fellowship with God. This is true for humanity as a whole and true for every one of us individually. Satan thought he had won and defeated God's plan for Jesus when Jesus died on the cross. Satan could not have been more wrong. The cross fulfilled not only the prophecies of the Old Testament but God's complete plan for our salvation. It is because of the cross that I can become the woman of God that I am designed to be and move in the fullness of authority and power.

God does not expect us to be perfect to complete his plan for us. He's already factored in the fact that we will make many, many mistakes. This is what allows God to be God.

Unbelief

The opposite of belief is disbelief, according to the dictionary. In Mark 9:17-24, there is the story of a man whose son was possessed of an evil spirit that rendered the boy deaf and mute:

> *17A man in the crowd answered, "Teacher, I brought you my son, who is possessed by a spirit that has robbed him of speech.*
>
> *18Whenever it seizes him, it throws him to the ground. He foams at the mouth, gnashes his teeth, and becomes rigid. I asked your disciples to drive out the spirit, but they could not."*
>
> *19 "You unbelieving generation," Jesus replied, "how long shall I stay with you? How long shall I put up with you? Bring the boy to me."*
>
> *20So they brought him. When the spirit saw Jesus, it immediately threw the boy into a convulsion. He fell to the ground and rolled around, foaming at the mouth.*
>
> *21Jesus asked the boy's father, "How long has he been like this?"*
>
> *"From childhood," he answered.*
>
> *22 "It has often thrown him into fire or water to kill him. But if you can do anything, take pity on us and help us."*
>
> *23 "If you can'?" said Jesus. "**Everything is possible for one who believes**."*
>
> *24Immediately, the boy's father exclaimed, "**I do believe; help me overcome my unbelief!**"*

77

Have you felt this way? "I do believe; help me overcome my unbelief!" I have - many times. I know that God's Word is true. I know that 'God is not a man that He should lie'. I know that there is 'no shadow of turning with God'. I know these things and yet, I still don't have the power of prayer and the absolute concrete belief that I need. I never question that God is able; I question, will He?

Unbelief is a hindrance to seeing our prayers answered. God understands when we have doubt and hesitation, but unbelief is unacceptable to Him. Unbelief denies the cross of Christ. Let that sink in for a minute. John 3:16 tells us that God gave His only son to die a horribly painful, shameful death nailed to two pieces of wood. God the Father allowed this out of His love for you and me. Jesus left the splendor of the heavenly realm and the continual presence of the Father to humble himself and come to earth as a human man, knowing that He would be the ultimate sacrificial Lamb. When I live or move in unbelief, it makes the sacrifice mean nothing. God forgives us because every one of us has done this at some point in time in our lives. The word repent means to 'think again' or 'think differently'. Repent and ask forgiveness right now of any unbelief in your life and ask the Holy Spirit to keep you away from unbelief. This is a hindrance that you do not want anywhere near you.

Here is a suggested prayer:

> *Lord Jesus, I know that You died on the cross for me and it was a painful, agonizing death. Please forgive me for the times that I have had unbelief in my heart. Help me to think differently and not allow myself to move into unbelief. I ask for a gift of faith to be deposited into my heart and I thank you for grace – unmerited favor – that allows me to come to You even when I'm in the wrong. Thank you for loving me so much! It is more than I can fully understand, but I am grateful for it every single day. Amen.*

Doubt

What is the difference between doubt and unbelief? The dictionary defines doubt as:

> *"A feeling of uncertainty or lack of conviction."*

I doubt my ability to do something. There is doubt about the authenticity of a historical document. I doubt my motivations. I doubt things will go my way. Doubt is also connected to hesitation. I am hesitant to step out in faith. What if I fail? What if I get it wrong?

Doubt can even come up as to whether God exists, or not. I have had times in life when I wondered. If God did exist, why did He feel so far away? What had I done to drive Him away? At this point in my life, I never have that doubt (I still have others). I have seen far too much evidence and answers to prayer and miracles to ever question if God exists.

God does not take offense at an honest question. You can ask the hardest things of life and ask Him if He's there. God will always respond to an honest heart seeking answers. It's also OK to be mad at God when hard things come. He is big enough to absorb our anger and love us through it.

However, God will never respond to any form of manipulation. If we seek to control God or get Him to do things our way or we feign an emotion in hopes of getting His pity, it will not work.

When God looks at us, He sees his beloved children and He sees all the potential and the blessings that He knows He put into the Book of Days for each of us. When we look at ourselves, we frequently doubt that we can ever be good enough to please God. This causes us to doubt ourselves and Him. However, *"His ways are not our ways and His thoughts are not our thoughts"* (Isaiah 55:8-9).

What we see in ourselves is our faults; He sees our potential and how much He loves us. Our world and culture have taught us to value different things than God does. He values me simply because I am His daughter. The world values me for what I 'produce', the value I bring, or the salary I earn. Those items don't even come into play when God thinks about us and how much value we have to Him from a Heavenly perspective. Our doubts are usually based on our judgment of ourselves and our shortcomings which we see as larger than life. God NEVER doubts. Period. It is not in His nature to doubt or to judge wrongly. We do both frequently.

To move from doubt to belief, we do have to repent – to think about things the way God does. We learn to do this by reading His word and asking the Holy Spirit to open our understanding of how to apply His Word in our every-single-day lives. We talk about 'coming into alignment' with God's Word. It is learning to value what God values and look at ourselves the way He does – with grace and love.

We must also live and walk in obedience to what we read. "Trust and obey, for there's no other way, to be happy in Jesus, than to trust and obey." (This is a childhood song by Don Moen) I will never get life right 100% of the time. Not this side of heaven. When I am doing my very best and relying on the Holy Spirit to lead me, living my life according to the principles in His Word, seeking Him daily for my provision, and honoring Him in all I do, I am and will be approved by God. Remember He already accounted for my humanness – that's why we have grace. (Read more about grace in Chapter 14)

A history of Fear

Fear is a God-given emotion, and it has its rightful place in our lives. Way back when Adam and Eve were in the Garden, fear did not exist. There was no reason for it too. Adam and Eve had awe and reverence for God, and they served Him out of love for Him. Not until they sinned out of disobedience was there a reason to fear and the need to hide. Can you imagine the moment Eve listened to the serpent and ate of the forbidden fruit, what that did to God's heart? God instantly knew the moment sin was committed. He knew the shift that had occurred and that there was no going back. I imagine him as a Father knowing his children had disobeyed and grieving in His heart over the punishment that had to be applied. If you are a parent, you have the insight to know the consequences and long-term impacts that your kids cannot know or see. How God's heart must have ached knowing what Adam and Eve's choices set in motion; the truth that the cross of Christ had become necessary for God and all people to be re-established in the relationship.

We do not know how long Adam and Eve lived in the Garden in peace before the fall. It was truly a time of innocence like nothing we can ever experience this side of heaven. Again, fear did not exist there. Neither did doubt or unbelief or jealousy or greed – none of the negative emotions were present. It was God's ideal setting for the human race.

After sin came, fear came. The serpent asked a 'simple' question – "Has God truly said…?" Satan planted the first seed of doubt and when that seed germinated, all the other negative emotions blossomed along with it: fear, disbelief, depression, loneliness, separateness, pain – physical and emotional, etc.

When God came to have fellowship with Adam and Eve after they sinned, the two humans hid from God because they were aware they had made wrong choices and disobeyed. They had fashioned coverings for themselves to hide their nakedness out of the first act of shame and regret. God sought them out – He came and found them, and they pulled

back out of fear. When God asked, "What have you done?",
Adam and Eve blamed each other – the first fight between
two humans – all triggered by doubt and disobedience which
led to fear.

Earlier, I said that fear is a God-given emotion. So, is fear
good or bad? It depends. It is the age-old quip, if you're being
chased by a bear, fear gives you the adrenaline to run faster
and get away. The natural response to a true threat to our
safety or our children's safety is a good thing – it helps save
lives. These are instinctual fears.

Fear of the Lord

The Word of God talks about fear of the Lord and it being
the beginning of wisdom. This idea of "fearing" God took
me a long, long time to understand and comprehend. It
confused me. How can I love and trust God and approach
Him and be in relationship with Him if I'm afraid of Him? I
just didn't get it.

I now interpret fear of the Lord as having tremendous
respect for God, knowing He is *the* God of the Universe. He
is also all-knowing, all-seeing, and is the ultimate perfection
of holiness, righteousness, and purity. There is not an ounce

of darkness or impurity in Him. He deserves every bit of respect I have and from that place of respect, I choose to obey Him out of my love for Him. He is the God of love, yes, but He is also a righteous judge and He has the right to hold me accountable for my thoughts, actions, choices, motives, and sin. He is immovable and what He has said is acceptable in his sight He will reward and what He said is not acceptable He will punish unless we repent of that sin and are washed clean by the blood of the Lamb. For me, the fear of the Lord is reverence and awe – I am not afraid of Him.

Mental and Emotional Fear

The last type of fear I want to discuss is mental and emotional fear. The stresses of life and the 'what-ifs'. Our 'normal' life contains far more stress that is imposed on us or we impose on ourselves than I believe God ever intended us to have.

I want to make a distinction between the stress of living – that of having a job, providing food for our families, being married, and including the stress that comes from relationships or being single and the stress associated with those challenges. It is not ever a right/wrong stress – it's the basic stress from being human and living on this planet.

However, so many of us, me included, add artificial and unnecessary stress on top of that. It's the stress from credit card debt. The stress of having 3 kids in 3 different sports at 3 different fields across town at the same time (not knocking sports here!). The stress of not getting enough sleep because you're hooked on that Netflix series and stayed up to 1 a.m. watching it. The stress of overcommitting to good things – church activities, volunteer opportunities, being on the Homeowners Association board, and the list can go on and on and on.

None of these are wrong or bad; we just have to learn to respect our limits and put our health first and not feel selfish about it. The artificial fear that we resist facing up to is the judgment of others who are also over-committed in many cases and it just perpetuates. The fear of missing out (FOMO) is a very real phenomenon. We get sucked into something that isn't necessary, but we've committed. Then we don't want to look like a loser by backing out, even when it's a drain on us and ultimately doesn't deliver anything we couldn't have lived without. I would ask you, what is more fear-causing; saying no to a 'good opportunity' and taking a chance on someone that you don't care about judging you OR explaining to your kids and spouse why you 'had' to be on that committee and will be gone for more time - again. We take our families for granted far more than we should. I am not saying we should not make commitments – I am saying not to over-commit especially when that excessive commitment drains life from you, creates stress, and leads to fear.

Sin

Sin is an obstacle to our relationship with God and sin can also be damaging to our mental, spiritual, and emotional health. Sin is going against what you know in your heart and your mind is right. What God calls sin is a behavior, mindset, or action that goes against the blueprint He created for the human race.

Adam and Eve's son, Cain, committed the first murder when he killed his brother, Abel, out of jealousy. As we just mentioned, when sin entered the Garden of Eden through Satan in the form of a serpent, the human race has had an inner conflict since that day. God goes on to say that not only those who physically murder others sin but if you commit murder in your heart, that also goes against the blueprint. It is from the motives of our hearts that our thoughts, words, and then, actions come. A dark heart will generate dark actions. In contrast, a heart with the light of Christ in it will generate more light and true freedom.

God also has said that *"ALL men have sinned and fall short of the glory of God"* (Romans 3:23 [Jesus is excluded from this, however]). God already accounted for our tendency to do wrong, and He made the Way for us to get back into relationship with Him. That's what Jesus did on the cross. So, if God knows we are going to sin, how can He hold that against us? It is when we are without Jesus as our Savior that our sin accuses us. Once we ask Jesus to forgive us and acknowledge what He did on the cross to save us, our sin no longer can be used as evidence against us. It's like it no longer exists in God's eyes.

I also don't think there are degrees of sin with God. The natural consequences we experience are going to vary based on what we do, yes. With God, we are either clean or we're not. It's that simple at its core. If I murder another person, I will go to jail for the rest of my life. If I tell my spouse a small lie about something, I may hurt his feelings, but the penalty is very different. With God and our relationship with Him, sin creates a barrier between us and Him that He CANNOT reach through. As soon as Jesus enters the picture, our sin is washed away, and God's hand reaches through the barrier and draws us into fellowship with Him.

I cannot call out all of the different types of sin nor do I want to. When you are not sure if something is a sin or not, ask God to show you. The Holy Spirit will teach and show you what you need to know. Boil it down to the motivation of your heart. Does it hurt you or someone else? Does it offend God? Is your heart motivation impure? 'Yes' to any of these questions? It is sin for you.

There is also the area where it may not be sin for you, but it causes someone else to sin or to be severely tempted. Out of pure heart motivation and love for that other person, don't cause them to fall and fail. Look out for the people around you just as you do for yourself. The goal is for ALL of us to live lives that produce good fruit and build up the Kingdom of God.

Journey Milestones:

1. On a scale of 1 – 10 with 10 being extreme unbelief, where do you find yourself on the unbelief scale? Think of your level of unbelief about how God sees you and how you see God. Again, be honest. God already knows but you have to acknowledge where you are to begin to change.

_____

_____

_____

_____

_____

_____

2. On a scale of 1 – 10 with 10 being extreme doubt, where do you find yourself on the doubt scale? Think of the doubts you have about yourself, your future, your relationship with Jesus, and the good plans He has for you. Again, honesty is a key here.

_____

_____

_____

_____

_____

_____

3. On a scale of 1 – 10 with 10 being extreme fear, where do
    you find yourself on the fear scale? Think of the fear you
    have for your future, fear of other people (people
    pleasing), being afraid of God, fear of the good/bad that
    is inside of you.

_____

_____

_____

_____

_____

_____

4. Sin separates us from God. Do you have ongoing sin that you need to deal with? No shame from God would prevent us from bringing our shortcomings to Him. He wants to have a deep relationship with you. Let it go....

_____

_____

_____

_____

_____

_____

Chapter 6: Choices and Decisions

How not to make decisions:

A married couple named Ananias and Sapphira made choices to lie to God and they died. This wealthy couple became Christians (at least, in appearance) in the years of the early church after Jesus had died. The church community was selling extra possessions and land to contribute to the community. Ananias and Sapphira agreed together that they would sell some property and give most of the money to the community but tell them they were giving all the money they earned. God knew the deception that was in their hearts and both of them died after lying to the Disciples. God immediately judged them, and they paid with their lives. This is a pretty extreme example, but it reminds us that God does take our heart motivations seriously.

Another man in the Old Testament started as a shepherd boy but grew up to become a King. David is known as a man after God's own heart, but David sinned greatly more than once. He had a man killed in battle so he could marry that man's wife. He and his new wife had a baby together, but that baby died from sickness. That was the consequence of their sin. King David repented and went on to serve God in many and mighty ways and wrote a good portion of the Psalms in the Bible.

We have many other examples of people who loved God but messed up along the way. They did experience the consequences of their choices but were used in significant ways!

Good Choices:

A man named Naaman in the Old Testament part of the Bible contracted leprosy. He had a slave girl who was a Hebrew (God's chosen people) and she prayed for God to heal Naaman. God gave the girl a message for the man to go and dip in the Jordan River seven times and he would be healed. Even today this would be a pretty far-fetched thing to ask someone to do.

However, after hesitating, Naaman did go to the Jordan River, dipped seven times, and was healed. From a significance perspective, this young slave girl is amazing. She must have had a good relationship with her master to want him to live. Naaman also is pretty amazing that he was willing to trust what this little girl said to do let alone trust her God.

A woman named Rahab was a prostitute in the city of Jericho. She helped two Hebrew men escape when they were discovered spying in the city. Because of her courage and assistance, her entire family was spared when the city of Jericho fell. Her actions were so significant they are recorded for everyone to read centuries later.

Choices face us every day and it's in the moment-by-moment, split-second decisions that our life's journey is played out. We often stew over significant decisions such as selecting a college, getting married (or not), having kids, accepting a job, changing jobs, divorce, purchasing a home, etc., and it's pretty easy to stress out over them. They are significant in multiple ways. They affect us at every level of our being, and it is right to give them thought and weight.

When Jesus needed to make important decisions, He got alone with the Father and poured his heart out to the One who loved him most. Jesus's heart was to accomplish the perfect will of the Father. Only through ongoing, personal conversation – talking and listening, could Jesus correctly discern the perfect will of the Father. God wants us to know His will for our lives. He does not keep it hidden nor does He want you to have to strive and search and search and search to find it. He will sometimes only reveal a portion of our future but that is done out of love to not overwhelm us. God is not a dictator that requires you to guess how many fingers He's holding up behind His back before He will tell you His best plans for you. He created you and He loves you beyond what our human minds can understand or our words fully express. He wants nothing but the best for each of us. What good would it accomplish for heaven and building the kingdom if He made finding out what we are supposed to do as difficult as possible? He does not think that way or work that way. That is not His character.

When we can't find what is 'right', it is almost always because we are not openly listening, or we go into asking with an agenda and an outcome we already believe is what we should do. Or, as so many of us do, we make a decision without asking and then ask Him to bless it or ask what happened when it goes sideways.

The good news here – nothing, I repeat, n-o-t-h-i-n-g we do or any choice we make will cause Him to stop loving us or offering us His grace and mercy. Even when we go off the deep end and get way out there…it only takes turning your face to Him and taking one baby step towards Him and He is instantly near you. He has walked me through more minefields of my own making than I care to recount. Every single time the outcome of asking for His help has provided a way through that was far better than what I ever thought I could ask for. Our God does not do things half-way. You are redeemed fully, not partially. You are saved fully, you are loved fully – flaws, faults, imperfections, skinned knees, and all.

Decisions:

Wherever you are in life today, you have decisions to make, big and small. What if you simply invite God into your decision-making process? Is there a catch? Yes, sort of. When God tells you there is a better choice than the one you want, what will you do? This brings us back to the topic of God's perfect will, His permissive will, or being *out* of His will.

I think of His perfect will like more of a straight line to get me from where I'm at today to where I need to be next. It's the most efficient way to accomplish what I need in my life to be the real, authentic person I'm designed to be (It may not be a straight line – that's just how I envision it for this comparison).

His permissive will allows me to wander off course but I'm still moving in the right direction. It just takes me longer to get there and there are usually delays and bumps and bruises along the way.

The final choice is to be out of the will of God. That's where we totally go into rebellion and *knowingly* make a bad decision for whatever reason. God will not prevent the consequences of any of our choices; He will offer grace and a redemptive path back to where we belong. There is no mistake, I repeat, no mistake that will cause Him to not allow us back and welcome us with open arms. Heaven is rooting for every one of us!

When God looks at you, He sees the potential and the gifts and abilities He lovingly placed within you when He spoke you into being. His offer to come back home always stands. He does leave the Light on for us. Always.

The most important decision you will ever make is to ask God into your life. The second most important one is to ask Him back if you've wandered off track. If you are reading this book and you have not ever connected to Jesus on a personal basis, here is a simple prayer for inviting Him and His eternal love into your life:

> *Jesus. I have heard about you and been reading about you, but I don't really know you as my friend. I want a personal connection with you, and I want you to be a part of my life. Jesus, please come into my life, into my heart, and make me clean. I know I don't always get it right and I've made mistakes in my life and I ask You to forgive me of all my wrongs. I want to experience the fullness of your love and get to know you in my everyday life. I know you are the Son of God that died on the cross so my wrongs can be erased, and I can have an eternal relationship with You. Thank you for loving me even when I have been so far away from You. Help me to receive Your love and grow in it daily. I want you to help me live the life You designed and planned out for me. Thank you, God. Amen.*

If you asked Jesus into your life just now, I want to celebrate with you! Congratulations – we are now related!! We are part of the family of God, and we get to spend eternity together with Jesus! Please go to my website and tell us about your experience – I have a free e-book to send you or mail to you to help you get started living with Jesus in your life. Go to my website at **http://www.lysabeltz.com/family.**

For many, many people, you went to church or Sunday

school as a kid and asked Jesus into your life. You experienced that joy. Then you grew up and life happened, and God wasn't top-of-mind anymore. You might pray when life got tough or you hit a lonely time, but it was not a priority. You have not even been sure God existed anymore. Maybe that was just a childhood thing. Now, you know you'd like Him back in your life but….

There are no 'buts' that Jesus has not heard from hundreds of other people – and He loves you in spite of every single one. Do not allow your 'thinking' self to talk you out of this. Your heart knows the truth. You want Jesus to come back into your life and you desperately want Him to be real and to be able to help make it all better. He can and He will! Here is a prayer to use as a start – add in your own experiences but just talk to Him and ask Him back.

Jesus, when I was younger, I know I asked you into my heart and I felt your love. I've wandered so far off and done so many things that don't line up with what you want for me. Please forgive me for the mess I've made. It's so hard to sort it all out. My head tells me one thing, but my heart says another. Jesus, I am asking you to come back into my heart, into my life, and help me get things back in order. I want you in my life. I want to live my life in a way that makes you happy and proud of me. I know you are the Son of God and you died on the cross for me. Please help heal my broken heart and put my pieces back together again. I need you. I want to live for you again from this day going forward. Thank you for your forgiveness and thank you for grace. I need lots of both! Change my heart and change my perspective so I can truly be happy and fulfilled. Amen.

The instant you began to pray, angels started rejoicing in heaven! We know that God loves all of us equally, but I do think He celebrates extra hard when we who drifted far off come back to him. He talks about celebrating over the one sheep that wandered off and was lost and he left the other ninety-nine sheep to go find the one. What a joyous occasion it is for Him! My prayer for you is that He replaces your tears of hurt, anger, bitterness, and loneliness with tears of joy and rejoicing.

Today is the beginning of a brand-new chapter – and maybe even a whole new book for you. I would love to celebrate with you and welcome you home – go to my website and drop us a note and I have a free booklet for you. Go to the website at **http://www.lysabeltz.com/renewed**. We have a God who planned our humanness and mistakes into planet earth and everything that was supposed to happen and is happening. He already accounted for the blunders we would make – they are no surprise to Him. Never even once did God think, "Wow, I didn't see *that* coming!" He has us covered.

Journey Milestones:

1. Everyone has made both good and bad choices. It's part
   of how we learn and grow. What we don't learn from, we
   repeat until we get the lesson. What good and bad
   decisions have you made that have significance in your
   life? Invite God into all of them, past and present.

   _____

   _____

   _____

   _____

   _____

   _____

2. What decisions are you facing today that you want God's
   input on? Ask Him and He will give you wisdom to make
   the best decision!

   _____

   _____

   _____

   _____

   _____

Chapter 7: Any vs. Every Road

"A man makes his plans, but the Lord God establishes them"
(Prov 16:9).

My Life's Plan

I have always thought and been taught that God has *A* plan
for my life, and I have to seek and seek to find *IT.* That held
me back from moving on some things for years.

Recently, God reminded me that He created me with a mind
and that I am designed and intended to <u>co-create</u> with Him.
This was a change to my understanding based on past
teaching. He wants us to partner with Him, not be dictated
to. I get to talk with Him and take my ideas to Him then I get
to speak it out and make it happen! *"A man makes his plans, but
the Lord God establishes them"* (Proverbs 16:9). God went on to
tell me that when I am walking in relationship with Him, the
things that are on my heart to do and accomplish are put
there by Him to begin with. My desire to write this book was

put on my heart in 2007. I had to live more years to have the necessary experiences before I could write about them. Here we are in 2020 and the book is published! In my career job of project management, I helped people accomplish their goals and vision for the company or their department via software systems. They told me what they needed to have happen and I went about making it so.

But when God asked me what *I* wanted; I didn't have an answer. I'm not used to being asked that question. I had to work through it for a while to really decide what I did want.

As wives, we work to support our husbands and families. As moms, we are focused on the best for our kids. Most of us neglect ourselves – or if not outright neglect, we put ourselves and our desires and dreams to last position just to get all the rest of it done. There is no condemnation in this. There is also no condemnation if this isn't you! I know amazing women who have the skills and capabilities and moxie to fulfill their dreams while raising a family. My hat is off to them! I didn't figure out how to do that.

Hints along the way

God did give me hints along the way. I will share two stories that happened years apart and years ago that I consider major milestones.

I was doing a part-time business with some friends from my church. Over time, the wife of the couple got to know me better and we had a great relationship. One day, she looked at me and said, "Don't you know you have a lot to say?" She saw in me what I could not see in myself at that time.

Years later, I was chatting with a speaker from Texas that had become a friend. After hearing him speak one night, I told him I knew I had significance and I was supposed to be sharing with other people, but I didn't know what my message was. He looked at me for a second and without hesitation he said in his Texas drawl, "Darlin', you are the message!" This fully resonated with my spirit, but I still didn't fully know what it meant.

I knew in those moments that what was said was important but, at the time, I didn't understand. I just tucked them away in my heart, trusting that God would show me at the right time.

NOW is that time. I do understand what I'm to be doing. I 'get' what it means for me to be the message – a lot of that is captured in this book. My life, my experiences, my walk with

God, my life, and His faithfulness in my life are the message. My mess is my message, and my test is my testimony. My ups and downs, faults and failures, successes and overcoming are all parts of my message and God will use them and me to encourage and help others.

God does not waste our experiences but redeems them all for His glory. We make life way more complicated than we need to. I can over-think a situation with the best of them – not that it has ever helped. God's ways are simple. Be who He made you. Like what you like, love what you love, do what you're good at – and do it in relationship with Him. When we have hearts that love God and we want to be in a good relationship with Him, life gets way easier.

The flip side is also true, however. When we are walking and living outside of a relationship with God, we get ourselves into some pretty deep and deadly messes.

Journey Milestone:

1. What hints have you received along the way that help point you in the direction of your goals and dreams? It may come from another person or it may come from God or something you suspect inside your heart.

    _____

    _____

    _____

    _____

    _____

    _____

Chapter 8: Unshakeable Beauty

A beautiful thing is never perfect. - Egyptian Proverb

Promise and Potential

When God is the Beholder and He looks at me and you, He doesn't see merely our outward, physical appearance. He sees us in the light of eternity – in the light of who He created us to be. He sees the promise and the potential that is inside of us. He sees our spirit and the light of Jesus that is reflected back to Him.

There is a child's song that talks about this: (*I am a Promise*, Gaither Vocal Band)

> *You are a promise*
> *You are a possibility*
> *You are a promise with a capital "P"*
> *You are a great big bundle of potentiality*
> *And if you'll listen*
> *You'll hear God's voice*
> *And if you're trying*

He'll help you make the right choices

You're a promise to be

Anything God's wants you to be

As a loving Father, his tenderness wants nothing but the best for us. Also, as a Father, He will bring instruction to ensure that we do grow up right. While we think short-term – today/tomorrow/next year – He thinks long-term about the next 50 years and our eternity. The beauty He sees in us lasts forever. He knows who we are at the core of our being – underneath all the layers and He says that woman is good!

Journey Milestones

1. How do you see yourself? What potential and possibilities do you recognize in yourself?

    _____

    _____

    _____

    _____

    _____

    _____

2. What labels do you apply to yourself in your mind and also how kind are you to yourself?

_____

_____

_____

_____

_____

_____

In Chapter 2 we talked about affirmations – I hope you are using them. Do you speak positively about yourself and acknowledge the potential that is within you? Do you see the possibilities in what you can do, accomplish, and become?

The only way to begin to change is to begin. Just start. Identify one action you can take today, that is a step forward. There's a great quote by Zig Zigler that says, "You don't have to be great to start but you have to start to be great." Another similar quote from Arthur Ashe puts it like this, "Start where you are, use what you have, do what you can". Change and progress are messy. Moving into living an intentional life can be messy. It's ok – it's part of the journey.

Mom-hair don't care! Sweats and a t-shirt? Doesn't matter. Make-up done, hair done, dressed, and out the door? Good for you. Don't let any of it be the excuse that stops you before you even begin.

Excuses never won a race, a prize, or brought growth. Set your mind – DECIDE that the shift starts now. You have potential or you wouldn't be reading this book. God has a purpose for your life and it's a good one. If you don't have confidence in yourself yet, borrow mine. I know that I know that I KNOW that you are meant to do great things with all God placed within you.

Lean on confidence in Him, too. The current dumpster fire you may find yourself in is made up of circumstances; it's not a life sentence. You are capable of change and you have that unshakeable beauty to guide you forward. It's there because God put it there. No one is an exception.

In the Old Testament, there is a scripture in Isaiah 61:3, that goes like this:

> *He gives beauty for ashes*
> *Strength for fear*
> *Gladness for mourning*
> *Peace for despair.*

I can have confidence in who I am and also Whose I am. I

am a blood-bought daughter of the Lord God Most High. He loved me enough that He sent Jesus to die on a cross so He and I could have an eternal relationship. Even when my life has gone up in flames and all that is left are the ashes, God gives unshakeable beauty for ashes.

God is a God of restoration. He takes the ruins of our lives – the dreams that went up in smoke, be it a relationship, marriage, business, wayward child, or what have you – and He gives back better than what we lost. Jesus didn't settle for anything less than the Father's BEST and we shouldn't either.

I could share many stories of people I know personally that God has done this for. In two examples, one woman experienced the loss of a spouse in a divorce, another woman the loss of a spouse to death. God brought the perfect person along for each of them and both newly married couples are exceedingly happy.

I have seen women whose lives were ruined by drugs and alcohol be restored to health, sanity, their children, and families all because of the love of Jesus. I have friends whose kids wandered off in their teenage years, but those kids have returned to have relationships with their parents. They are not perfect, never will be – but where they are is better than they ever imagined.

Journey Milestone:

1. What beauty do you need and want to be restored to your life?

_____

_____

_____

_____

_____

_____

2. What do you need to forgive yourself for?

_____

_____

_____

_____

_____

_____

Kindness Matters

Another way we exhibit beauty is through kindness. Kindness is so very needed in our world right now. I have never met a kind person who didn't demonstrate beauty to me. In dramatic contrast, I have never seen a person with inner beauty who had an outright lack of kindness.

Kindness is grace applied to someone or a situation where calling out a fault or flaw would be so easy to do. It's quietly tucking someone's tag in the back of their shirt; it's giving someone fifty cents when they are short in the grocery line instead of impatiently tapping your toe for them to get out of the way. Kindness looks like picking up a mom's cell phone she dropped while juggling a baby and a sack full of groceries. Kindness looks like quietly slipping a boy on a date $10 when the girl orders something more expensive than he planned on. Kindness is giving that person that dresses, looks, and talks so different than you a smile when they're having a bad day. Kindness shuts down judgment because judgment shuts down relationships.

Every single person alive today has the choice to be kind or not. Be kind and teach others to do the same. If it is to be, it's up to me. Start a kindness ripple wherever you are. You will never regret being kind.

Journey Milestone:

1. What kindness ripple will you commit to starting? Be creative! The smallest act of kindness creates great ripples.

_____

_____

_____

_____

_____

Fruits of the Spirit

Unshakeable beauty starts and ends in your heart. It is that non-tangible element that makes you attractive regardless of what you look like. It's the spark, the sparkle, and the light in your eyes that makes people stop and do a double-take. This beauty does not fade with age – it gets deeper, richer, more mature, and even more attractive. If you had a grandmother that you admired and looked up to, think of this beauty as what made your grandma special.

In the New Testament book of Galatians, in Chapter 5 verses 22 – 23, God tells us that the fruits – the results of living in His Holy Spirit – are Love, Joy, Peace, Patience, Kindness, Virtue, Faithfulness, Gentleness, and Self-Control.

> *But the fruit produced by the Holy Spirit within you is divine love in all its varied expressions:*
> *a joy that overflows,*
> *a peace that subdues,*
> *the patience that endures,*
> *kindness in action,*
> *a life full of virtue,*
> *faith that prevails,*
> *a gentleness of heart, and*
> *strength of spirit.*
> *Never set the law above these qualities,*
> *for they are meant to be limitless.*

Entire books are written about the Fruits of the Spirit. Let's look at definitions from the perspective of inner beauty.

LOVE – the Holy Spirit moves only in love and He sets the

example for us. When we are in a relationship with Him and allow Him to guide our motives, we operate from a beautiful place of love for our fellow man beyond what we can manufacture ourselves.

JOY – This is an active joy – a bubbling-up-and-spilling-over-from-the-inside kind of joy.

PEACE – when your soul and spirit are at peace, the lines around your eyes soften and the corners of your mouth want to turn up not down. This is accompanied by a deep sense of being OK.

PATIENCE – never quitting, never giving up on yourself or others.

KINDNESS – a sweetness of spirit that genuinely looks out for and wants the best for others.

VIRTUE – goodness that follows you around and rubs off on all those around you.

FAITH – an overcoming belief that all will turn out well despite the odds or what you see at the moment. This is also an active faith – it jumps right into the fight or fear and sends them packing.

GENTLENESS – an intentional humility in life, a tender

thankfulness to God with active compassion for others. It can also be a quiet, controlled strength.

STRENGTH OF SPIRIT – sometimes also written as self-control. It is being in control of your mouth and your emotions and using your superpowers for good, not the destruction of others.

When we have Jesus and the Holy Spirit, we will see more and more of these fruits or results in our lives on a daily basis. The desires we have often change and what is of real importance is what we want to focus on. Even a person's outward appearance will change. There is a new spark of life in a woman's eyes, a softness in her face, a quick smile, and a radiant spirit that can't help but shine for others to notice. The harshness is gone and replaced by quiet confidence and a new outlook on life.

Journey Milestones:

1. Which of the above characteristics do you want to develop more of in your life? Be specific as to what it looks like in your day-to-day routine. Pick, at most, three, and plan out what action steps would get that into your life.

_____

_____

_____

_____

_____

_____

2. Describe your inner beauty. This is often the hardest
   assignment in the world! List a minimum of five things
   about yourself that make your personality and spirit
   attractive.

_____

_____

_____

_____

_____

_____

Chapter 9: Abandon the Ugliness

The Dark Side

Do you know that part of you, that side of you that you try to keep hidden from most people? We all have her. The dark side of our souls. The person within us that is harsh, judgmental, snotty, gossipy, selfish, angry, bitter, or jealous (just to name a few traits). Most of the time, we are able to manage and keep this part of us hidden from view. However, some women lead with this side of themselves and do so with pride!

That is not me at the core of who I am. When I am overly tired, stressed, outraged, severely out of food, or way out of my comfort zone, a part of me emerges that I generally don't like and don't see very often.

Did you also know that we have 4 sides to our personality? They are:

1. The part of me that I and everyone else sees – my public personality

2. The part of me that everyone else sees but I don't – my blind spots

3. The part of me that only I see – the inner me

4. The unconscious part of me that is unknown

Johari Window

	Known to self	Not known to self
Known to Others	Arena	Blind Spot
Not known to Others	Facade	Unknown

This description is called the Johari Window (Joseph Luft and Harry Ingham, 1955). I want to look at part two, our blind spot because that's usually where our weaknesses or flaws stand out whether we are aware of them or not.

As we discussed in the last chapter, it is your inner spirit and kindness that make you beautiful. Conversely, it is the lack of inner peace, inner kindness, and love that makes us ugly and unpleasant. I discovered I had self-hatred, self-loathing, and self-condem-nation inside me that tainted and discolored everything I saw in myself. It caused a lack of confidence. It caused me to doubt everything about myself. I held back because I didn't want to be seen. I played small in life because I was sure others would agree with me that I was unworthy.

Tracing this back, it started in my early teenage years – those hard years of 13 – 15. For me, it was 7th and 8th grade – Junior High. I didn't fit in. I was 'different'. I was a 'smart kid' and so many of the things everyone else laughed at simply were not funny to me. I loved God even at that age and spent hours reading my Bible. I was a bit of a loner even with a few good friends. Somewhere along the way, I accepted that I was different and would likely always be different and I was OK with that…mostly.

When we feel ugly from the inside out and don't like ourselves, we have a hard time accepting that Jesus could possibly want anything to do with us. How could He have a good plan for us and certainly there's no way He would want to use us for anything significant. But the TRUTH is, He does! Our behavior and even the way we see ourselves do not diminish what God has planned for our lives. We do have to change the way we live our lives by asking for forgiveness of our wrongs and when we do, Christ has a way of accelerating our path and getting us back to where we were meant to be all along.

Results from the Dark Side

In the last chapter, we looked at Galatians 5 and it showed us the 'fruits of the Spirit'. Also, in that same chapter, it tells us the results and outcome of living by our human nature – the negative fruit we produce. It says,

> *"19 The cravings of the self-life are obvious: Sexual immorality, lustful thoughts, pornography,*
>
> *20 chasing after things instead of God, manipulating others; hatred of those who get in your way, senseless arguments, resentment when others are favored, temper tantrums, angry quarrels, only thinking of yourself, being in love with your own opinions*
> *21 being envious of the blessings of others, murder, uncontrolled addictions, wild parties, and all other similar behavior."*
>
> *Gal. 5:19-21 TPT*

When we are consumed by living for nothing but ourselves, it gets easier and easier to hate ourselves more and more which just makes continuing down that wrong, desperate path easier and easier. This is where we become ugly. We see nothing good in ourselves and often, nothing good in anyone else either. If we do see the good in someone, we ridicule and hate them because we're jealous. Hopelessness, depression, and despair become our constant companions. Fear is also never far away. If you've been here, I'm sorry. I pray you've found a way up and out of this muck. If you haven't – there is good news for you. Jesus is the ladder up out of the pit, regardless of how or why you got there. You have hope and a future when Jesus enters the picture. He will wade right into whatever mess you're in and walk with you all the way out. Jesus is not afraid of you, your sin, your fear, your ugliness, jail, prison, drugs, alcohol, abuse, illness, addiction to prescription pain killers – there is no ugly He won't approach and show you the most amazing love you've ever experienced. He will not leave you in your pit IF you will take His hand and receive the help He offers. Here is where you get to "Abandon the Ugly".

Journey Milestones:

1. What is the ugly part of yourself that you are ready to let go of? What is the motivation behind those emotions?

_____

_____

_____

_____

_____

_____

2. Write your younger self a note of forgiveness. Let her know she is loved in spite of her flaws and recognize she did the best she could with what she knew at the time. If tears come, let them flow and do their cleansing work.

_____

_____

_____

_____

_____

_____

I Want Out of the Pit

One other thing to be aware of – we never really fully 'arrive' at not needing Jesus. Whether you're in a pit or a palace, we are always going to be human and that means messing up. The Bible tells us that ALL have sinned and fall short of the Glory of God. The Bible also tells us that God never condemns us – He never makes us feel ashamed or judged for the stupid, wrong things we do.

The Holy Spirit will 'convict' you, meaning, he'll point out in His gentle way where we are off course and need to fix our attitudes, motivation, behaviors, and make better choices. God brings correction to our lives to make us better. Other people and the enemy of our souls, Satan, will bring accusations that make us bitter and feel worse. God always calls us forward to do better. Satan reminds you of your past and lies to you that you will never amount to anything. Listen to God – He brings life, not death.

If you are in a pit of any kind, here is a way to pray to ask for God's help getting out and moving towards a better life.

> *Jesus, I am so far down in a hole I can't see a way up or out. I don't like myself. I don't like the choices and decisions I've*

made, and I want out of this, but I don't know-how. I am
asking you to come and help me. I need a path forward. I need
a flashlight to show me the way in the darkness. I cannot do
this by myself. Will you come right now and show me You are
here? I am sorry for all the messes I've made in my life that got
me here. I want to change, and I ask for Your help with that,
too. I need you in my life. Please come now. I believe You are
God, and You have the ability to give me a hand up and get me
into a better place. Thank you for hearing me pray. Amen.

Jesus is faithful – He will show up every single time when you
pray an honest, heartfelt prayer like this. There are no magic
words you have to say – just be blatantly honest with Him.
He knows you and your situation anyway – we can't hide
from him even though we think we can. God looks at what
we mean in our hearts – our inner-self, not our words. That's
why the words don't matter as much as meaning what you
say. There is a power that comes when we call on the name
of Jesus. It is unlike anything else you will ever experience.

If you are not in a pit but know you are off track and God
has shown you some ugly in your life, pray something like
this:

Jesus, I see that I am wrong and not where I need to be in

_____ area. I ask You to forgive me and wash away the ugly

and replace it with Your love which is pure and unconditional.

Show me any other areas of my life that I need to clean up, too.

I want to be the woman You created and designed me to be and

this sin does not contribute to that. Help me keep my heart

tender before you so that I sense and respond to the prompts of

the Holy Spirit, so I stay on track. Lead me back to the place

I'm intended to be and give me peace and joy for the journey.

Thank you for your faithfulness to forgive me and love me

always.

Chapter 10: The Yoke

What is a yoke?

The definition of a yoke in the dictionary (Dictionary.com):

1. A device for joining together a pair of draft animals, especially oxen, usually consisting of a crosspiece with two bow-shaped pieces, each enclosing the head of an animal

2. Something resembling a yoke in form or function, such as a frame fitting over a person's shoulders for carrying buckets suspended at either end

3. An immense, oppressive force or burden - *under the yoke of a tyrant*

Here are pictures since this is not something familiar to most of us.

Figure 2 A Yoke of Oxen

Or

Figure 3 Water Pail Yoke

When we are carrying the weight of responsibility in our lives, it can feel very much like a yoke that we are saddled with. Paying bills, raising kids, taxes, rent/mortgage, marriage, being alone, divorce, death, job responsibilities – there is no end to the list of things that can weigh us down and cause a sense of being overwhelmed. Some would say this is just life. It just goes with the territory. It's easy to assume we are alone to deal with what we experience from the inside out. Even if you're married, your spouse cannot feel what you are feeling.

But Jesus can. In the first book of the New Testament, Matthew, in Chapter 11 verses 29 and 30 Jesus tells us,

> *"29 Take my yoke upon you and learn from me; for I am gentle and humble in heart, and you will find rest for your souls 30 For my yoke is easy, and my burden is light." (NRV)*

Another translation says it this way:

> *"29 Simply join your life with mine. Learn my ways and you'll discover that I'm gentle, humble, easy to please. You will find refreshment and rest in me. 30 For all that I require of you will be pleasant and easy to bear." (TPT)*

Because Jesus is with us all the time, He knows exactly what we are experiencing. He doesn't have to, but He offers to share the load with us at all times. The idea of being 'yoked' with Jesus is that He will help carry the load – we do not have to do it alone. If we will give it up, Jesus will carry the heaviness that weighs us down and He will take on the largest part of the weight. This does not mean we don't still work and care for our families, but it does mean we can worry less and seek out His wisdom for every circumstance we are in.

Journey Milestones:

1. We often carry weights and responsibilities that are not ours to carry. What yokes can you identify that you need to take off and let go of and give to Jesus to carry?

   _____

   _____

   _____

   _____

   _____

Religion vs. Relationship

Another meaning of the Matthew 11 scripture is that Jesus will never demand of us to carry a heavy load because of Him. For me, *this is where religion and relationship differ greatly*. Religion that is not based on the love of Christ can feel very heavy and demanding. Religion is man's attempt to reach

God.

Relationship, in contrast, is God reaching down to us out of pure, unconditional love by sending Jesus from heaven to come to earth as a man. As a man, Jesus feels all the emotions, knows the struggles, the heartache, the temptations, the joy, the pain – everything it means to be human.

In spite of being fully human, He never sinned. He never made a wrong decision. He never told a lie. He was never rebellious. All because He knew the bigger picture that God the Father was working to accomplish. Jesus surrendered his life to death on a cross purely out of His great love for us. He overcame sin, death, hell, and the grave because we never could.

When Jesus offers for us to be yoked with Him, it is from His position of victory and overcoming. He already won! Because He is God, He can walk with every single believer on the face of the earth at the same time and not get tired.

> *"He, watching over Israel, slumbers not nor sleeps,"*
> *Psalms 121:4.*

When we are yoked with Christ, it is very different than any other relationship we will ever have. Jesus is always and forever FOR YOU. Two oxen in a yoke together cannot choose to go two different directions. You always put an experienced ox with a young ox to 'learn the ropes'. When we are willing to be that younger ox and allow Jesus in His wisdom and experience to teach us and guide us, the path is easier, the burdens lighter, and we don't make stupid mistakes.

So, what appears as a bad thing, being in a yoke, is a good thing when we are yoked to the Savior. Alternatively, if we chose another yoke-mate, the way is generally a much harder go. If your yoke-mate is anything or anyone but Jesus, you just have to ask for His help and be willing to make the changes He shows you. Ask Him into that partnership right now...

> *Jesus, I am tired of carrying all the weight, responsibility, and burdens on my shoulders. Your Word, the Bible, says that you offer to share the load and bring me joy and rest. I would like that very much. Please come and be my yoke-mate. I also ask for help to make the changes I need to make. Guide me in my decisions so I can walk next to you for the rest of my life. Thank you. Amen!*

Journey Milestones:

1. If you have experienced the weight of religion, people's expectations, and their demand to conform you to their standards (not the Lord's), write them down and then give them over to Jesus. (Note: not all religious practices are wrong or out of line. Many of them are highly enjoyable and life-giving. Look for the ones that weigh you down, shut you down, or don't allow you to be yourself.)

_____

_____

_____

_____

_____

_____

Chapter 11: Resilience

Life is FOR me

Remember my poster from Chapter Four?

> *"Don't pray for an easy life,*
> *Pray to be a strong person."*

While I wish some of the difficulties in my life had never happened, I genuinely am grateful for the strength in my character and my spirit. Life does happen. It's a matter of does it happen TO us or does it happen FOR us? What's the difference? I'm glad you asked.

We are made and meant to participate IN life, not have it happen to us. You are stronger than you think you could ever be. There is an internal fortitude, the ability to persist, persevere, bounce back, recover, and regain your footing that you may not know is there. You CAN do this! Then, when you add Jesus to the situation, you become unstoppable.

Jesus said, *"I (Jesus) have come that you may have life and have life more abundantly"* (John 10:10). It means to have a life with joy and strength for all the aspects of you - spirit, soul, and body. God did not EVER intend for us to merely survive life. He fully intends for us to enjoy life with joy, love, acceptance, and a relationship with Him.

Will there be difficulties? Absolutely. Will lots and lots go wrong? Guaranteed. Is life messy? Most always. However, He walks <u>with</u> you through every crappy situation, providing grace and provision of people, finances, material things, a place to live, food, etc. No, God is not a vending machine or a genie. He IS a good Father and will bring what you NEED, and often what you want, too.

When life does happen TO you, and it will, you always have a choice. You can become bitter and resentful and carry the baggage of those circumstances with you and let it weigh you down. The other option is to forgive, work through it, learn the lessons, and then move on.

For me personally, my husband and I went through a period of life where we pretty much lost everything we owned – none of which was my fault.

I CHOSE to take the high road, not walk away from the very undesirable situation I found myself in with a 3-year-old at the time. Was it gut-wrenchingly hard sometimes? Damn straight. Were there times I wanted to run, not walk away? Yes. Did I cry a lot? Yes, A LOT! Did I live to talk about it? Also, yes. Could I have done it better? Maybe. Nothing prepares you for the unexpected.

For twenty-five years I have looked back and beaten myself up second-guessing decisions I made and thinking how much better I 'should' have dealt with it all. Keep in mind, this was overwhelmingly massive and messy. No, I should not have handled it better. I did the absolute best I could with what was available to me at the time. My coping skills had to come up to speed fast. My resilience was tested for several years in a row. And I passed. I kept my family together, paid the bills we could pay, I leaned on other people over and over and over. I did not go through this alone, manage it alone, or carry it alone. There are a handful of people that I will be eternally grateful for. I could not have made it through without them. Likewise, you do not have to do this alone.

Jesus and the Holy Spirit.

As I have mentioned in a prior chapter, this difficult season of life was where I learned to lean on God and to pray, to intercede, to rely on God because, at times, there was nothing else to do. When Jesus says He is an ever-present help in times of trouble, He means just that. 24/7, 365 days a year. He never waivers, He never ceases to be there, and his love never fails. I proved Him and took Him at His Word, and He delivered.

Resilience is Learned

If you are not resilient today, you can be. If life has failed you once, more than once, or a bunch of times, today is a new day. Those experiences were where you learned the lessons. Now you get to apply the learning and CHOOSE differently. Your words, your thoughts, what you really, truly believe at the core of your being are the things that determine how resilient you will be. If you repeat to yourself daily, "I can't do this!" or "This is too hard for me", or "I am such a loser!", you won't be able to do it, it will be too hard and you will lose, again.

If, however, you will change your self-talk and say something like, "This is shitty-hard but I can get through it!" and "I am facing large challenges but the things I need to get through this are on their way to me and I will succeed!", "I am learning and growing every day", "with God's help, I will get through this." If you repeat these phrases OUT LOUD multiple times a day, every day for a couple of weeks, the shift WILL come. The things you need will show up; connections, finances, a place to live, the map of the minefield, a job, a babysitter, a business. God's got you! Ask Him for his goodness to be poured out and then begin to thank Him that it's on the way! If you miss a day, start up again. If you don't see the change yet, keep going! Continue to believe and look for the changes to come. They will. God will match your energy and your gratitude. If what you're putting out is positive, positive will come back. If you put out gratitude, supply will show up.

Not only are you resilient, but life is, too. I can tell you story after story of women and men of all ages who have made sweeping changes in their lives in a few months. It may not be an overnight change, but the first shift can happen in moments.

Journey Milestones:

1. Where in your past or present have you felt life was against you or taking from you rather than being for you?

_____

_____

_____

_____

_____

_____

2. What area do you want to ask God to build resilience within you? Ask Him to partner with you in building muscle in your mind and determination.

_____

_____

_____

_____

_____

_____

Chapter 12: Purity of Heart

"Blessed are the Pure in Heart, for they shall see God." Matthew 5:8

Bible Study How-to

We are going to take a little detour here for a minute or five and talk about ways to study the Bible. Some of you will want to dig deeper into different translations, different languages, and even the context when certain things were written. There is so much to learn and a lot of great information and tools available. Knowledge is power and the more you understand, the more powerful you will be at applying all you learn.

If this is not of interest to you right now, move onto the **Pure Hearts** section later in this chapter.

One definition of the Bible that I love is **B**asic **I**nstructions **B**efore **L**eaving **E**arth. It is God's wisdom written down to help us live our best lives. God thought up, designed, created, and wired our DNA. He knows how we humans are intended to work better than anyone else can. He gave us the Bible as our Survival Guide.

For many of us, the languages in older versions of the Bible are hard to read and even harder to understand. Thank you, God, that different people have updated the language into our words and phrases. Both The Message Bible and The Passion Translation as well as the Amplified Bible boil it down to simpler phrases and terms in modern language or add explanations. Even with those translations, you sometimes want to go deeper. There are online courses and books that will teach you how to study the Bible. I will not go into that detail here, but I do want to tell you about a couple of websites that I find useful, and I want to show you how I use them.

BibleHub.com, BlueLetterBible.com, and BibleGateway.com all offer different versions of the Bible that you can select from a drop-down menu.

Tip #1: Look at verses in a couple of different translations to get the different ways the original language can be interpreted. The Old Testament was written in Hebrew and the New Testament was written in Greek.

Some words from Hebrew and Greek have multiple words in English that can mean similar things. They are, typically, very similar but give you a more well-rounded look at what the original intention was when the verse was written. For example, look at Matthew 5:8 in different versions:

The Passion Translation *"What bliss you experience when your heart is pure! For then your eyes will open to see more and more of God."*

The Message Bible: *"You're blessed when you get your inside world—your mind and heart—put right. Then you can see God in the outside world."*

New King James: *"Blessed are the pure in heart, for they shall see God."*

Amplified Bible: *"Blessed [anticipating God's presence, spiritually mature] are the pure in heart [those with integrity, moral courage, and godly character], for they will see God."*

A Literal Greek Translation: *"Fortunate those free in the heart, because they themselves will see for themselves the Divine."*

The different looks give you a well-rounded meaning of what God meant in this verse.

Tip #2: Use a reference book like Strong's Concordance which is also listed on those websites. Each word in a verse may have a number next to it [2513] which is a cross-reference to the Strong's Concordance where you can look up that word and get its different meanings. Start simple and just use Strong's. There are other Bible commentaries that can be explored too but don't lose sight of what you are trying to learn in the first place.

Here is Matthew 5:8 with the Strong's reference #'s showing:

"Blessed[G3107] are the pure[G2513] in heart; [G2588] for they shall see God [G2316]."

To use the Strong's Concordance, look for how to show 'reference' text or use Strong's and it will insert the [number]. These numbers are clickable and will drill down into the original meaning(s) of the language it was written in.

For this example, let's drill down into the word 'Pure' [G2513]. What does it mean to have a pure heart? Why does God value it?

Strong's Concordance defines "pure" as clean, clear, pure in simple terms. Going into more detail:

- clean, pure, unstained, either literally or ceremonially or spiritually; guiltless, innocent, upright
- 513 katharós (a primitive word) – properly, "without admixture"; what is separated (purged), hence "clean"

(pure) because unmixed (without undesirable elements); (figuratively) spiritually clean because purged (purified by God), i.e. free from the contaminating (soiling) influences of sin.

Another reference text has this definition:

- …Ethically; free from corrupt desire, from sin and guilt: free from every admixture of what is false, sincere

From all of this, we get a picture of what that one verse implies that we don't see by just reading the words. This is why thousands of people spend their entire lives reading and learning from the Bible. There are so many nuances and details that we lose sight of. Many things are references to the culture that Jesus lived in that we simply aren't aware of unless we read about it. Jewish customs and traditions that were their normal, daily lives are unfamiliar to us.

Pure Hearts

Ok, that was more of a detour than I thought it would be… (P.S. It's totally fine if you skipped all the stuff above for now – just start reading again HERE.)

Let's get back to talking about pure hearts and why that

matters.

When my heart (my emotional center of my being) is full of anger, resentment, bitterness, or unforgiveness, my entire view of the world, of other people, and God is shaded and distorted. I have an agenda. I want revenge. I want whoever did me wrong to pay!

In this state of mind, it's impossible for us to accept God's unconditional love and we certainly will have a hard time loving anyone else. We are apt to be pretty harsh and foul-mouthed with our words.

The Bible tells us that *"from the heart comes all of our words and motives"* (Matthew 12:34, Luke 6:45). God is not willing or able to bless us when we operate in this mode.

I think of it like sending your teenager to their room when they have a horrific attitude, "Come back and talk to me when you can be nice". We still love them, but we don't like them very much right then. God's the same way – He always loves us, but He doesn't have to tolerate our bad attitudes.

When you're tired of being grumpy and bitchy all the time and you don't like what the ugliness inside is doing to you, guess what?! You get to choose to change! This is where we have a heart-to-heart convo with God and tell him we are wrong, ask for His help to change, and ask His forgiveness.

In Psalms 51, King David put it this way, *"Create in me a clean heart, oh God, and renew a right spirit within me."*

Here is a simple prayer to get you started:

> *Father God, Jesus, I don't like the way I'm living. I don't like my attitude or the ugliness in my heart. I am full of anger, bitterness, resentment, and unforgiveness and it's killing me from the inside out. I want to change. I start by asking You to forgive my sins – the things I do wrong. Please create a new, clean, pure, softer heart in me. Wash away all the grime and grit from the past and let me start over again with a new way of being. I want to live differently but I know I can't do it on my own. Would you please come and help me? I believe You have a better way for me to live and I ask You to lead me into that. Thank you in advance for all the good things you have planned out for me. Amen.*

Let the tears fall – they, literally, release the bitterness out of your body. Let the Lord wash you with His love. When we ask God for a new beginning and we mean it, God immediately starts things in motion to make changes for you – both inside and out. He will purify your heart, your motives, your attitude, and your outlook on life. Some of it will happen quite quickly, other parts over time.

When we are walking and living from a place of having a pure heart, there is an emotional shift that takes place. Those absolutely annoying habits of the people you love, and strangers, both seem less impacting. Things that used to cause you to swear just don't ruffle your feathers anymore. You feel lighter in your step. Your ability to heal from the inside out becomes a real possibility. The absence of bitterness allows joy to come and take over. They cannot co-exist in your life. If you've ever had fish tanks, you know you cannot have a single tank that is both fresh water and saltwater at the same time – it has to be one or the other. Similarly, you cannot be bitter and joyful simultaneously.

*"Blessed are the pure in heart for they shall **see** God."* (Matt 5:8) When you operate in that pure heart, you see God every day, everywhere, in everything. God's hand is on your life, guiding, providing, encouraging, and correcting. Beyond seeing God in everyday living, you will also hear His voice, feel the nudges of the Holy Spirit, and be blessed with His Presence always.

In this verse, the word "see" literally means 'to appear, to be seen, to behold'. It is possible to have an honest-to-goodness visitation from Jesus. Ask for it – seek it. You will never regret making yourself available for Him to come to visit you. It is life-changing! The peace, the assurance, the knowing that you are loved is beyond description. He WANTS to have that level of relationship with you. Accept His invitation to be in a relationship with Him and to grow in Him daily.

Journey Milestones:

1. Purity of heart is achieved instantly when Jesus makes it clean. The ongoing lifestyle of maintaining a pure heart is where we need the Holy Spirit every day. Write down your pledge and commitment to yourself and to God of what you will do to stay in touch with the Holy Spirit.

    _____

    _____

    _____

    _____

    _____

2. When you ask to see God and grow in your relationship with Him, what will that look like for you on a day-to-day basis? Relationships grow when you spend time investing in them.

_____

_____

_____

_____

_____

_____

Part 3: Becoming Unshakeable

Years ago, when my husband was looking for a name for his business, we prayed about it and asked God for a name. I knew our daughter was supposed to help in the naming process. When I asked her what she would name a business, she had no idea, but she grabbed a dictionary. The dictionary opened to a page where she was drying a flower and the word at the top of the page was, 'Groundwork'. Part of the definition said, "It takes a lot of groundwork to build a solid foundation" and thus, Groundwork Consulting was born.

Parts One and Two have lain the groundwork of knowing who I am and how God works in my life, what the challenges and obstacles are, how to overcome them, a basis for making decisions, overcoming fear, doubt, unbelief, and much more.

Part Three builds on that foundation and gets us on the action path to becoming unshakeable in life, inside our heads, and in our hearts.

Chapter 13: In Step with the Holy Spirit

"We are the home of the Holy Spirit – we carry him with us everywhere."   *1 Cor 6:19*

One Step Away

I was driving on our local freeway on the way to a business luncheon and I was asking the Lord if I was on or off track with where He wanted me to be in my life. Somehow, I expected a lecture and a bullet point list of all the things I needed to change. Instead, what I got was, "You are only ONE STEP away from being in alignment with Me."

In my own perspective, I tend to go spiritual four-wheeling pretty often – headed out to the wilderness to do some more off-roading again. As I drove on the freeway, He showed me that the lane I was in was parallel to where I needed to be. I was going in the right direction, at the right speed, in the right vehicle; I just need to shift over one lane to the left of me. This was true, literally, for where I needed to go as well as symbolically in my spiritual walk.

If you grew up in church, it may have felt like it was so hard to "find God's will for your life". As an adult with a lot of years of walking with God, I have concluded we make it way too difficult and way too intellectual. When you are honest with yourself, deeply honest, you know what you are good at and what strikes passion in you. God made you exactly the way you are naturally with abilities, skills, and talents. He wants you to use those things to do good in the world and bring honor to Him. Everything you do from the most menial task like cleaning a toilet to cleaning up a child's puke can be done with a heart that loves God. Your job, your family, your sense of humor – all are made to bring joy to you and Him.

It is also true that it is a life-long journey to become all that God intends you to be. Each new age and phase of life brings new discoveries about who God wants and needs to be in your life. The three-year-old you needs a different aspect of God than the thirty-three-year-old you or the sixty-three-year-old you. When we walk with the Holy Spirit as our guide, He is always faithful to open the doors we need opened and close tight the wrong ones… IF and WHEN we choose to partner with Him, ask His guidance and be willing to listen to the small nudges in our spirit when they come.

Holy Spirit in Me

How do we walk with the Holy Spirit? The Holy Spirit lives in us as soon as we invite Jesus into our life. When Jesus left earth to return to his Father in Heaven, the Holy Spirit came to the earth and empowered 120 people who had been followers of Jesus (read the Book of Acts).

As those 120 shared the good news of the gospel of Jesus with other people, when they believed in Jesus, they also received a relationship with the Holy Spirit. The Bible tells us that *"our bodies are the home of the Holy Spirit and He resides within our spiritual hearts"* (I Corinthians 6:19). This is part of why Jesus had to leave earth and go back to Heaven – so that the Holy Spirit would come to live with every believer. Again remember, when Jesus was here, He was a literal man and could only be in one place at a time. The Holy Spirit is able to be with all people at the same time.

And remember, the Holy Spirit has always existed along with the Father and with Jesus. In the book of Genesis, the Holy Spirit is mentioned in chapter 1, verse 1:

"1 In the beginning, God created the heavens and the earth. The earth was without form and void; and darkness was on the face of the deep. 2 And the Spirit of God was hovering over the face of the waters." *(Genesis 1:1–2).*

The idea of the Spirit 'hovering' over the void is like a picture of an eagle spreading its wings over its nest to protect her eggs or chicks from a storm. That is still how He cares for us, too.

Frequently, the Holy Spirit is represented as wind or breath which we see again in Psalms 33:6:

"By the word of the Lord the heavens were made, and all the host of them by the breath [Spirit] of His mouth."

It was also the Holy Spirit who breathed life into Adam when God first created him:

"And the LORD God formed man of the dust of the ground and breathed into his nostrils the breath of life; and man became a living soul." *(Genesis 2:7).*

The Holy Spirit comes to give us life – new and fresh when we get stagnant – He can and does breathe new life into us. This is yet another way that God shows us His love.

In Psalms 32:8, the Holy Spirit is shown to be our teacher:

"I will instruct you and teach you in the way you should go; I will counsel you with my loving eye on you."

Another Greek word for the Holy Spirit is 'Paraclete' which means counselor, advocate, comforter, or helper. It's important to know all the roles that Holy Spirit fills to empower us to understand how we can walk better with Him. One thing God will never do is ask us or tell us to do something that is out of line with His character. When we learn about his character and how He operates, it's easier to tell when 'advice' or guidance we hear does not fit with what God would have us do. For an extreme example, the Holy Spirit would never tell you to rob a bank to pay your bills.

Journey Milestones:

1. Do you know if you are on track with where God has directed you in life? If you do not feel like you are, what one step of adjustment will you make to get closer to and into God's path?

_____

_____

_____

_____

_____

_____

2. Whether you've known God for a long time or if you
    have just recently invited Him in, right now, ask the Holy
    Spirit to make Himself known to you. Sometimes, people
    get chills, feel a warmth in their heart, or sense a
    Presence. Pause and just quietly listen for his voice of
    encouragement and guidance. Record what you hear and
    your experience.

_____

_____

_____

_____

_____

The Holy Spirit as My Counsellor

"But the Counselor, the Holy Spirit, whom the Father will send in my name, he will teach you all things, and bring to your remembrance all that I have said to you." John 14:26

The men and women who lived at the same time as Jesus and who loved Him immensely did not want him to leave. Jesus was only thirty-three when He died on the cross. However, God's plan all along was that Jesus would return to Heaven and the Holy Spirit would come to live continuously with the believers who followed Jesus's teaching. It brought the disciples great comfort to know that God would be with them, although, at that time, it was a brand-new idea, and they didn't know what to expect exactly. The believers and followers of Jesus who received the Holy Spirit were not only comforted, but they were also given the ability to partner with Holy Spirit and do great miracles.

The Holy Spirit is available to us just like He was for the early believers. When we face difficulties in life or even in reading the Bible and making sense of it, the Holy Spirit will bring understanding and wisdom to us. Something you've read twenty times and didn't get, all of a sudden, it's like your eyes are opened and you DO get it! That is the counsel of the

Holy Spirit.

The Holy Spirit as an Advocate

> *"I will ask the Father, and he will give you another advocate to help you and be with you forever—the Spirit of truth."*
>
> *John 14:16-17*

What does an advocate do? An advocate helps you speak for yourself, so your needs are heard, your rights are represented, and you get a resolution to your problems. 'Advocate' can also be a legal term, which is also a significant place where the Holy Spirit acts as our legal advocate or our defense attorney with Satan. Satan is an accuser and is our adversary. Satan wants to stand before God and remind God of all of our failures and shortcomings. His is that voice you hear in your ear reminding you that you are not good enough. This is NOT the voice of the Holy Spirit, our advocate. The Holy Spirit reminds us that we are clean before God because of what Jesus did on the cross. The Holy Spirit will always remind us of what Jesus accomplished and that Jesus died for you and me. The Holy Spirit acts as our defense attorney with Satan in this sense. He advocates on our behalf and reminds Satan that we belong to God.

The Bible tells us that Jesus is an advocate for us, also. Jesus prays (advocates) for us continually before the Father and the Holy Spirit as Counselor guides us into truth and realization of ALL that is ours because of what the Cross accomplished.

The Holy Spirit as a Helper or Comforter

With God, we find safety, security, and comfort that sustains us in this life and beyond. These words of King David from The Passion Translation express it well,

> *"Because you are close to me and always available, my confidence will never be shaken, for I experience your wrap-around presence every moment."*   *Psalms 16:8*

Even if you don't "feel" Him, you have the eternal Comforter giving us His "wrap-around" presence every moment. We're covered by the comforting blanket of Christ wherever we go. The Holy Spirit is in fact, the "Spirit of Christ" or the "Spirit of Jesus" because the Holy Spirit is like Jesus.

Here are two verses that show us more:

> *"God, your wrap-around presence is my protection, and my defense…" Psalm 7:10 (TPT)*

> *"Whether you turn to the right or the left, your ears will hear a*

voice behind you, saying, 'This is the way; walk in it'."

Isaiah 30:21

We are in a relationship with the Holy Spirit. The more time you spend in the Word of God, the more you will know Him. The Holy Spirit will use our Bible reading as an opportunity to commune with our spirit and teach us. Consequently, we need to give space to the Spirit as our teacher who was sent that we might understand the things freely given to us by God (1 Corinthians 2:12).

Journey Milestone:

1. Which aspect of the Holy Spirit do you most relate to right now in life: Counselor, Advocate, Helper, or Comforter? What do you need the Holy Spirit to help you with in that role?

_____

_____

_____

_____

_____

_____

Chapter 14: Submit and Surrender

"All to Jesus I surrender, all to Him I freely give…"

(lyrics from 'I Surrender All')

The Lord has said these two words, submit and surrender, are not popular words in this day and age. People do not like to be told what to do and we rebel against submitting to authority. That authority represents parents, bosses, the government, pastors, teachers, administrators, God, and anyone who could ask or tell us to do something that we might not like. We resist rules. We want to do what is best for ourselves or perhaps ourselves and our families. This also applies to believing in and following the rules of life outlined by God in the Bible.

Submission by Demand

There has absolutely been an abuse of power by many in authority in every area of our lives. This is true in our churches just as it is anywhere and everywhere else. People fail us. They just do. That does NOT mean that God is the same. God is very clear in His Word that He is different:

"I am not a man that I should lie." (Number 23:19)

"My ways are not your ways; My ways are higher than your ways." (Is 55:8-9)

"Having no other name by which to swear, He swore by His own name – I AM that I AM." (Exodus 3:14)

When we are hurt and abused by people, especially those in churches who profess to be Christians, it can make us want to turn our back on God Himself. It's easy to think, "If those people represent God, I want nothing to do with any of it." I have heard and seen this play out over and over in my years of following Christ. I did not 'grow up in church' but I have been a Christian since I was nine years old. That has given me several decades to observe and learn pretty much all flavors of how this works out.

People feel offended by others and walk away. If that is you, I am genuinely sorry for the harm that was done to you. Sometimes, it is people with good intentions and motives that are just off base. Other times, people have wrong motives and are absolutely in it for themselves and still others are blind to how they have wrongly impacted those around them.

I would ask you to think about the fact that it was the 'religious leaders' of the day who crucified Jesus. They were more committed to their human traditions than they were to being open to what God Himself was doing on the face of the earth.

God IS love and He loves you unconditionally – even right now today wherever you are and however you are. When God asks us to submit to His ways, He does so with nothing but pure motives. He does not ever manipulate or have an ulterior motive other than what is best for your life. I ask you to consider giving God another chance. Just you and Him. No one else interfering in the middle.

Take time right now, whatever you're doing, and ask Him if He's real and would He show up for you in a real, authentic way. Some people see what we call 'God Winks': a hummingbird, a dragonfly, a bluebird, a coin on the ground that says, "In God We Trust", etc. Others see white feathers, or a friend calls them out of the blue just to say," Hi". God knows what is in your heart and He's fully good with it. He is a big enough God to not be put off or offended by your doubts, anger, hurt, or even disbelief. If you will engage with Him honestly, He will respond every single time, with no exceptions.

Submission in Love

When God asks me to submit to Him, it allows me to come
under his protection and authority. Think of a baby chick
running under the hen's wings when it is hailing. Hard balls
of ice falling from the sky can take out a chick. By submitting
to the protection and covering of the momma hen, that chick
can weather the storm and come out unhurt. God offers us
that same option. We are not and do not become a zombie
when we walk with God. He created you to be exactly who
you are. He wants nothing more than for you to be yourself!

There is a difference between "having our own way" and
"being our authentic selves". God does expect us to follow
the Bible and live the way He designed us. This is also where
you have to decide and go all in or dabble around the edges.
Since God created man – God holds the original patent and
has the blueprints – then He knows best what makes us tick,
what makes us happy, what brings joy, and also what damage
poor behavior and wrong living do to us. It's a whole lot
easier to submit to God when you see Him as having your
best interests in mind than to an image of God that is distant,

uncaring, and only wants His way.

When I was about twelve years old, my dad and I were up early one Saturday morning, which we often were. It was Mom's day to sleep in. My hands were cold (as usual). Dad was making coffee on the stove in the really old percolator-type coffee pot. He had me come over to him and grabbed both my hands and was pushing them towards the coffee pot! I have to say I freaked out a little! I didn't understand what he was trying to do! My fear was getting my hands burned and I momentarily forgot how much he loved me. He stopped when my hands were about four inches from the pot – and I felt the warmth from the coffee pot on my skin and my hands instantly were warmer. I think I was crying and probably trying to pull away. All he was doing was being a caring dad and showing me a way to warm my hands.

God is the very same way. He loves and cares for us and has good intentions towards us. Even when we don't understand and we pull away, He is driven by nothing but love for us and warming our hearts and our hands.

Journey Milestones:

1. What has been your past experience with the idea of God? A distant, far-off, uninvolved God? A judgmental God waiting for you to fail? Someone you didn't want anything to do with? Or didn't feel good enough for? Record your experience and thoughts.

    _____

    _____

    _____

    _____

    _____

    _____

2. Take time right now and ask God to show up for you in a real, authentic way. Regardless of what your past is or your past experience with God – be honest and transparent with Him about your fears, your needs, and your desire to know more of Him and more about Him.

    _____

    _____

    _____

    _____

    _____

    _____

3. What can God be for you in this season of your life and current circumstances that He could not be before? Do you need hope, faith, healing, direction, forgiveness – He will come right to where you are and give what you need most. Record what you need Him to be.

_____

_____

_____

_____

_____

_____

Surrender

From this basis of God being a loving, compassionate, caring God – let's also talk about surrender.

In war, the side that surrenders is the loser. When a fugitive surrenders to the law, they feel they have lost. Any kind of a fight or battle or squabble where we 'surrender' to something, we typically feel we've lost. One of the definitions of surrender says this:

Surrender: abandon oneself entirely to (a powerful emotion or influence); give in to.

Even this definition can be taken positively or negatively. You can surrender to anger or you can surrender to love. When God asks us to surrender, it is to surrender to His unconditional love. This idea of surrender to God is, again, not becoming a pre-programmed zombie whose constant response is "Yes, Master. Whatever you say." God created you to be YOU and He is delighted in who you are! He designed you exactly the way you are, and He wants you this way. His love sees only the potential in you – the potential He put in you before you were ever born.

Are you totally messed up right now? Ok. He loves you and will help you turn that mess into a message. Are you pretty together right now? Great! He will take you as-is and make you a powerhouse. Are you living a pretty rough life and kinda way out there right now? It's OK. You are only one step away from being on the right life path.

The first step for all of us is to choose to surrender to the love of God. Does surrender sound like a weak move or showing vulnerability to someone you don't trust? It takes more strength and faith to take a baby step in surrender than it does to keep fighting. Coming into alignment with God is NEVER a weak move. It is a shift in strategy, it is a shift in position, and it is a shift in how you will see yourself.

Journey Milestones:

1. What are your initial thoughts and reactions to the idea of surrendering to God? Does it create peace, fear, doubt, hesitation, hope, or ____? Do you have a positive or negative idea about the concept of surrender?

_____

_____

_____

_____

_____

_____

So, what does this look like in real life? Let's think about the extremes for the sake of highlighting the contrast.

Self-Motivated:

When I am all about myself, I make decisions that benefit me without consulting anyone or considering the impact on anyone else. I may tell myself the lie that I'm doing it for others but deep down, I am "self" motivated. I can find ways to justify my actions however hurtful they may be to myself or others. Drug users, alcoholics, shoplifters, addicts to power or money, people with eating disorders, and people addicted to working out excessively find the means to justify it in their minds. They feel they are in control while, actually, the thing they focus on controls them. They may regret hurting the people around them, but it does not change their behavior or actions.

God-Motivated:

Contrast that to living a life surrendered to God – letting Him be in control. When we ask for God's forgiveness for our sins and believe that Jesus is the Son of God, we enter into a relationship with Him and we have access to all the wisdom God possesses when we ask him out of sincerity and honesty. He wants us to be successful in life. He wants nothing but the best for us. He knows what makes us tick and He will help us identify where we need to change, things we need to let go of, things to start and stop doing, and what fits best with how He made us. What does the Bible say about this?

In 2nd Timothy 1:7, we see this verse:

> *"For the Spirit God gave us does not make us timid, but gives us power, love, and self-discipline."*

Another scripture is Romans 12:2.

> *"Don't copy the behavior and customs of this world, but let God transform you into a new person by changing the way you think. Then you will learn to know God's will for you, which is good and pleasing and perfect."*

Proverbs 3:5 – 6 puts it this way:

> *"Trust in the LORD with all your heart; do not depend on your own understanding. Seek his will in all you do, and he will show you which path to take."*

When we are willing and able to surrender to God's love and choose to live with Him directing our everyday lives, magical things start to happen. I don't believe in luck or coincidence. Instead, I see God-appointed meetings, divine timing, and connections. We happen to run into someone looking to hire a person with our exact job background. We find the money we had forgotten about and it's the exact amount we need to pay a bill. You can't explain how, but the money in your checkbook covers everything you need through the end of the month, someone gives you new clothes that are perfect for your interview and the list goes on and on. All of these things have happened to people I know personally.

Our surrender brings God's favor into our lives. A friend of mine always says, "I am God's favorite, just like you." And it's true – we are all God's favorite, and He loves to pour out His favor on us.

To be sure I don't make this sound like it's all cotton candy and flowers, surrendering to God is not always easy and not always comfortable. It is a life-long journey and is where the original title to this book came from: "The Journey to Becoming". I updated the title to *Becoming Unshakeable* as the book evolved.

Grace

Every day is a new chance to live the best way or the self way. Some days we do good and others we don't - it's just part of the human experience. This is where the idea of grace comes in. Grace is God's undeserved favor and blessing when we are human, which is all the time. God does not expect us to be robots or to be perfect. He didn't design us that way. He gave us intelligence and minds and a will and desire, and He wants us to use those things the right way. He didn't create you to love the color blue then punish you when you love the color blue. He does not operate that way.

One example of grace in action is when I tell a lie to cover up something I shouldn't have done. Our mouths and our words get us into trouble probably more than anything else on the planet. When I get that nudge inside that reminds me I did wrong, I can ask forgiveness from God and His grace covers my sin. I may also have to tell someone else that I lied, and I will have to deal with any outcomes. Grace doesn't always take away the consequences.

Trust and Obey

Besides submit and surrender are the concepts of trust and obey. God will sometimes ask us to do things that we don't immediately understand or see the reason for. When you are certain it is God asking you do something, you take the action to step out in trust and you obey what you heard.

I was driving home from work one day and God specifically

told me to drive on different streets than I normally do. I didn't see why but I did it. Did I avoid an accident? Probably. Or maybe God was seeing if I would listen so He could give me more significant instructions in the future.

I have also been prompted to walk up to a Wal-Mart employee and ask if she needed prayer for something. Of course, she did, and she was a believer. She was so very grateful I listened to that prompt.

One day at work, the Lord told me to go for a walk outside in the afternoon. I headed out and He reminded me to go grab my sunglasses. As I walked, He directed me to turn right or left at certain streets and I ended up in a park where He showed me a sign that was posted there that had meaning and significance to what He was showing me.

Trust and obey are not going to be flashy things or always life or death matters – but sometimes they are that, too. Another funny thing that happens sometimes is I will be impressed to wear a specific color and go to meet a friend and she's in the exact same colors. It's just fun!

I also have to add that God has quite the sense of humor. So many of us grew up with this image of God sitting in a Heavenly Courtroom with a gavel in his hand just waiting for us to screw up so He could throw the book at us. To be clear, there is a Heavenly Court; however, once Jesus is in your life, He is your defense attorney, and He defends you, not condemns you.

Back to God's sense of humor. We are told that we are created in God's image – we have a sense of humor and therefore, so does He. In Proverbs we are told that *"laugher is like a medicine"* (Proverbs 17:22). Think about a baby or a child's laughter – such pure joy it just warms the heart. I also think about the contrast of a giraffe to a corgi dog and just laugh at the leg contrast! What makes you belly laugh or laugh so hard you cry? It is such a natural reaction to the things that tickle our funny bone. It just has to be God!

Psalm 2:4 says *"God, who sits in Heaven, laughs."*

In Jeremiah 31:13, *"I will turn their mourning into joy, I will comfort them and give them gladness for sorrow."*

And again, in John 15:11, *"'I have said these things to you,'" Jesus said to his disciples, "'so that my joy may be in you, and that your joy may be complete'."*

In Matthew 18:3, *"Truly I tell you, unless you change and become like children, you will not enter the kingdom of heaven."*

If the sound of a child's laugh is one of the happiest sounds to us, it is to God as well. He LOVES to hear that laughter from them and from us. Laughter, joy, gladness, happiness all shows us that God values lightheartedness.

Submit and surrender, trust and obey and laughter. At first glance, those words are not connected but, with God, all things are possible.

Journey Milestones:

1. Are you more self- or God-motivated and why? Do you want to remain that way? Why or why not?

    _____

    _____

    _____

    _____

    _____

    _____

2. Being willing and able to trust a God we cannot see is a huge step of faith. What are your thoughts right now about trusting God? Can you and do you trust Him? If you don't yet, are you willing to have relationship with Him to find out if you can trust Him?

_____

_____

_____

_____

_____

_____

Chapter 15: We are an Endangered Species

Those Who Pray

When God gave me the title for this chapter, I was like, what? At the time of writing this book, according to the ever-knowing Google, there are 7.594 billion people on Planet Earth. Again, according to Google, 1/3 of those people identify as Christians. Of that 2.5 billion worldwide, the portion in the United States (233 million) who pray every day is about half or 116 million. While that still sounds like a lot of people, that number has been going down every year over the last ten years.

Does God care about how many people pray to Him? Do we have to pray every day to be followers of Christ? What is God looking for in those who follow Him?

This is a challenging topic. I will do my best to outline what I hear from the Lord around this and share His thoughts and His heart as I understand it.

God is looking for pure hearts. He is looking for individuals (women and men of all ages) who will set aside their agendas, opinions, priorities, politics, power plays, fears, and doubts and be the people God made them to be and work with Him to be the face of God and the face of good on earth. These are the type of people that God says are becoming an endangered species on the face of the earth.

Does God care if we pray every day? Yes, He does. If you are married – what happens when you go days without speaking to your spouse? You get disconnected. Misunderstandings happen and a distance can form. If you're a parent with kids at home, same thing. We typically don't go a day or days without conversing with our littles.

Prayer is not always a formal thing where you bow your head, fold your hands, and recite some prayer. Prayer is a daily, ongoing conversation with the Father, Jesus, and the Holy Spirit. We are encouraged to "Pray always, without ceasing". Talk to God when you're changing a diaper, changing your oil, washing dishes, running, running an errand, lifting at the gym, anytime and all the time. When you make every day an ongoing conversation with God, you grow close to Him. You learn to hear and recognize His voice. He talks to every one of us in a way that is significant to us.

What God sounds like to me is different than it is to my husband. We can get the same message, but God will present it differently and use different ideas to get us to the same place. He knows us as individuals. He does not shout from Heaven and expect everyone to hear the same thing. He does not dictate and expect us to take down His words in shorthand (is shorthand even a thing anymore?).

If we only "pray" when we need something, we can end up treating God like a genie or a vending machine. That's not how it works. I often find that prayer is more listening than it is talking or asking. If I can be quiet and listen for the voice of the Holy Spirit – what some call The Still, Small Voice – I receive instruction, inspiration, answers, solutions, and questions to think about.

Praying in Purity of Heart

In a portion of the New Testament book of Matthew called 'The Beatitudes', Matthew 5:8 tells us, "Blessed are the pure in heart for they shall see God". We did a study on the word 'pure' in Chapter 12. Jesus tells us that to be pure in heart is to be like a little child. They do not have malice or judgment in their hearts – they are accepting of life around them and ready to learn more.

Another way we can be pure in heart is to tell God our wrongs and ask His forgiveness. Jesus says that He washes our sins completely away and He does not remember them any longer. He buries our wrongs in the deepest part of the ocean and leaves them there.

Once we ask forgiveness, that sin or wrong can never be held against us. We do wrong things every day which is why part of our prayer should be to ask God to show us what we need to ask forgiveness for daily. It keeps our hearts clean and pure so that it doesn't create a barrier between us and God. In Proverbs 4:23 we read,

> "So above all, guard the affections of your heart, for they affect all that you are. Pay attention to the welfare of your innermost being, for from there flows the wellspring of life."
>
> *in this scripture, "heart" refers to our thoughts, our will, our discernment, and our affections.*

Here's another question for you... How do I know what I need to ask forgiveness for? I mentioned in an earlier chapter that B-I-B-L-E stands for Basic Instructions Before Leaving

Earth. By reading the Bible and, in particular, the whole New Testament plus Psalms and Proverbs, we get an understanding of what God loves and dislikes. Keep in mind, we are designed and created to function best when we love what God loves. Just as you need food and water (and for some of us, coffee) daily to stay healthy, you need the Word of God – the Living Bread – daily.

We work our physical bodies at the gym to get and stay strong, and we need to pray and be in God's word frequently to keep our spiritual selves healthy and strong. It also helps keep you sane. When we read about how many times God rescued other people throughout history from their troubles, it gives us peace and confidence that God will help in our lives, too.

Journey Milestone:

1. What comes to mind that you need to ask forgiveness for?

_____

_____

_____

_____

_____

2. Will you commit to praying every day? It is an ongoing conversation with God. Sometimes it can look like quiet time on your knees but don't limit it to that.

_____

_____

_____

_____

_____

Endangered

To be considered an endangered species, a species has to be at risk of extinction because of a rapid decline in population or loss of critical habitat. When God said that His people who have genuinely clean and pure hearts are an endangered species, He was referring to both criteria in the definition.

As discussed at the start of the chapter, the number of Christians worldwide has declined over the last decade. In some countries, it is a crime punishable by death to profess to follow Jesus. There are at least, fifty nations where converting to Christianity, having a Bible, or simply being a Christian is punishable by beating or even death. We are fortunate in the United States to still have the freedom to worship as we choose. There are other areas where it is harder to be a Christian but is not outlawed.

I don't bring this up to be negative, but to highlight our disappearing environment. We live in a world and a time with a lot of darkness. Jesus told us clearly that this would happen in the last days before He returns to earth. God's Word tells us that Satan comes as a thief to steal, kill, and destroy. He is hell-bent, literally, on defeating God. The way he does that is to come against those who love God and Jesus and who listen to the Holy Spirit. He is our sworn enemy whether we like it or not and whether we believe it or not. Our enemy HATES Jesus with a wave of anger so deep we cannot comprehend it. He will stop at nothing to break Jesus's heart. Satan has no respect for anyone or anything. He is full to the brim of evil and there is no redemption for him ever.

While this is a bit sobering, I have some really, really great news – Jesus has already won the war with Satan! If this was a sports game, our team is so far ahead on the score that with the time remaining in the game, the other team cannot score enough points to catch up. We are just playing out the rest of the clock.

When Jesus died on the cross, Satan thought he had won but after three days when Jesus rose from the grave having defeated death, not just for himself, but for all generations, Satan realized his absolute error and defeat. He knows he is playing from a loss position so he has nothing to lose by going all out and taking out everyone he can. Jesus tells us to use His name and the enemy HAS to leave. When, not if, you are harassed by Satan's minions, speak the name of Jesus and command them to leave you alone. We have no power in our own name but *"at the name of Jesus, every knee must bow, and every mouth confess that Jesus is the Son of the Living God"* (Philippians 2:10-11).

James 4:7-9 says,

> *"7 So then, surrender to God. Stand up to the devil and resist him and he will turn and run away from you. 8 Move your heart closer and closer to God, and he will come even closer to you. But make sure you cleanse your life, you sinners, and keep your heart pure and stop doubting 9 Feel the pain of your sin, be sorrowful and weep! Let your joking around be turned into mourning and your joy into deep humiliation."* (TPT)

This again talks about the importance of keeping our hearts pure and staying in constant contact with God every day.

God is Bigger!

To conclude this chapter, we need to also realize that regardless of how hard the devil works to defeat God, God is bigger, has more resources, and has already won the war. The outcome is decided. God needs people with pure hearts that He can live in and work through to bring goodness, salvation, and relationship to every person possible. God desires that everyone joins Him in heaven. He does not want even one person going to hell. People who reject Jesus are not allowed to enter heaven. It is that black and white. For all God's mercy and grace, He has a minimum requirement for people to be saved, and the only way in is through His Son. The price that Jesus paid by suffering and dying on the cross bought our entrance to eternity with God.

If you've hit this chapter and are not sure if you have access to heaven through Jesus, below is a prayer to ensure you do!

> *Jesus, I now know that you are the one and only Son of God and that You died on the cross so I can be in eternity with You. I recognize you as my Savior and I ask you to forgive my wrongs that I have committed up to this point in my life. Please wash my heart and make it pure so that I may see You. I want to live a life that is pleasing to You and I want to be your partner in getting others into heaven for eternity. Thank you for going to the cross for me and thank you for forgiving me. Teach me Your ways and help me to think more like you think, act live you act, and love as You love. In Jesus' name I pray, amen.*

Journey Milestones:

1. What is prayer to you? A quiet time of meditation?
   Talking to God throughout your day? Praying over your
   family for provision and protection? What will you do to
   include more prayer into your life routine?

   _____

   _____

   _____

   _____

   _____

   _____

2. Part of prayer is listening to God and then praying out
   loud for the things He shows and tells you about. What
   do you hear God telling you to pray over right now?

   _____

   _____

   _____

   _____

   _____

   _____

No Longer a Guest; We Are Family

You are family to the Lord. We have access to Him, and we have the Keys to the Kingdom. As soon as you ask Jesus into your life to be your Friend and Savior, you become family to Him. Jesus, the Son of God, graciously gives us a place next to Him at the family table as his sister or brother. In legal terms, we become joint-heirs with Jesus. We inherit the Kingdom of God right along with Him. This still amazes me to this day!

In the Jewish tradition that Jesus lived in and grew up with, once a son was old enough to join the family business, the father announced in a public setting that this son was now legally able to do business transactions on behalf of the father. It was like adding "& Son" to the business name and adding the son to the business checking account. The son could write checks out of the business checking account now. The amount the son quoted for a job was as binding as if the father had named the price. This gave that son authority.

God has done the same thing for us. When we accept Jesus and actively live our lives in agreement with the Father, we are given authority as sons and daughters to move and speak on His behalf. When I tell a minion of the devil that he has to

191

leave, I do so with that God-given authority as a daughter of the King. When I pray for a sick person and declare life and healing for them, I do so in the authority given to me by God. Every person who names Jesus as Lord has this same authority. This is not a special thing only for pastors or church leaders or older people. But, just as there are different levels of authority in business or government, there are different levels of authority here, too.

As you grow in your understanding of the Word of God and you learn His ways, your levels of authority will also grow. You don't let a three-year-old child try to ride a racehorse. You give that child a pony to help him begin to learn. When that child has graduated from a pony to a larger horse and his skills increase, eventually he can handle a racehorse.

Listen to the Holy Spirit and He will guide you and teach you. We grow and learn by doing. Begin to pray for people and situations around you. You will see what works and bring adjustments to what doesn't. It is also good to pray scripture for and over people and circumstances.

The Olive Garden restaurant chain had a slogan for a while that said, "When you're here, you're family". People who are followers of Christ should have this same attitude towards one another. We may see and believe certain things differently but if we look for what we have in common, which should be a love of the Father, Jesus, and the Holy Spirit, we need to treat each other with sisterly (and brotherly) love. Families don't always get along and certainly don't always agree but there should always be a basis and foundation of love. 1 John 4:16 says,

> *"We have come into an intimate experience with God's love, and we trust in the love he has for us."*

God is love! Those who are living in love are living in God, and God lives through them. Let God's love live through you.

Journey Milestone:

1. Spend some time thinking about what it means to be a daughter of a King. You are royalty, you are treasured, and you are loved. How does this change how you see yourself?

Chapter 16: Becoming

Be all you can be!

The weight of God's glory (His majesty, grace, and goodness – how amazing He is) does not weigh us down; God buoys us up! The Bible tells us that we can be covered by and rest in His glory and then we become enabled and empowered to go and do what He has called us to. It is through surrender that we are sent out. It is heavenly logic, not earthly logic. He uses the weak to confound the strong. We cannot will or force a person to be changed or healed but when we are surrendered and allow His will to be carried out through us, the blind will see, and cancers will fall away, and the dead will be called back to life.

You get more of what you focus on.

When I say, "Don't think about a white mouse", what do you immediately picture in your mind? A white mouse. Our brains are wired TO think about things; they don't understand "not". It's like having a car that only knows forward – not reverse. Our brains only can focus on the thing itself.

When I say, "I am so broke" or "I am so sick" or "I can't lose weight", we are telling our brains that what we want is to be broke, sick, and overweight. Instead, re-train yourself to express and focus on what you do want. "I am completely able to pay my bills", "I am healthier every day", and "I am closer to my ideal weight every day". This instructs your brain to move forward towards what you thought about.

Dr. Caroline Leaf has spent much of her career researching brain function from a scientific standpoint. She is also a Christ-follower and is seeing scientific research catch-up to and validate scripture over and over. I highly recommend her book "Switch on Your Brain" if you need a process to help you reformulate your thinking.

When Jesus was teaching, He always gave positive instructions – "Follow Me", "Repent and sin no more", "Come to Me..." etc. He did not say, "Don't follow John" or "Don't be a fisherman anymore".

Jesus also said, "Ask of Me and I will give you...". How many times could we have had a different outcome if we had asked for help, health, provision, to change our thinking, for grace, or for a blessing? We are often taught to be independent and self-made. It is part of what we in the USA cherish as a culture. However, the downside to this approach is disappointment, burned-out workers, unrealistic expectations of ourselves and others, suicides on the rise, divorce at the highest level ever, abuse everywhere we look, and the list could go on. To change our world, we have to start with changing ourselves and those we have influence on. Asking for help does not mean the other extreme of relying on everyone else to do your part. It is asking for and expecting what you need to fulfill your mission on earth – and we all have one.

God knows the how.

When God asks you to do something, He already has the HOW figured out. Because we like to be in control of our destinies, we usually focus on "How am I going to do that? Then, when we can't do it, we move into that negative mindset of, "I don't have enough 'x' to do what God told me to do. I must have heard Him wrong".

We talked in Chapter Two about being in the Flow of

Heaven. When we are cooperating with God and in the place that He needs us to be, He already has provision figured out. However, in order to get us to the place we need to be with the right faith, mindset, and focus, He will use challenging circumstances to teach us reliance on Him. It may take months or even years of apparent "lack" where we have to rely on God for our source of provision to build the character He needs in us to take on the bigger assignment we were being prepared for. He has to know that our integrity will hold up when the kitchen is empty and our kids are hungry. The groceries you desperately need will show up from sources you never expected and your immediate need will be met. This builds your muscle of reliance on God and your personal experience that He does come through for you. Once that muscle is strengthened, the assignments will grow bigger and the impact and consequences greater. While God will never tempt us, He will try us to see if we're ready for the next bigger thing. Your job during this time is to do the next right thing.

Resist the urge to think small.

When I was fresh out of college and just starting a career, I wanted what I called a 'baby Mercedes'. The one I pictured in my mind was a classy grey color. I have never owned or even come close to owning that car because I talked myself out of it. "I don't really need that." "I don't deserve that." "Maybe someday I'll have a car like that." The underlying message to myself was one of denial, not only of the car but assuming that any motivation I had for wanting it was wrong and bad.

Fast-forward a lot of years and I have come to realize that having a desire for nice things or a 'fancy' car does not put me at odds with God. I do not have to have and maintain a poverty mindset to be approved by God. Somehow, somewhere along the way, I picked up the theory that having less and going without made you more holy. Now, let me say immediately that there is no judgment or condemnation against or about anyone who is challenged financially. If you have chosen to live with less – perhaps so one parent can stay home to raise kids or so you can go to school, there is absolute honor in that. I also recognize that other situations such as health issues or where you live will dramatically impact your ability to change your circumstances. God has been, is, and will continue to move in your life and bless you.

I am speaking to those of us who have accepted less because of a wrong belief system or a victim-minded mentality. I believe it is not possible to have a poverty or scarcity mindset AND accomplish all the things God has put me on earth to do. If I am going to impact my world for Christ and to spread the gospel, it takes finances, prosperity, and the right mindset and belief system.

God created us to win.

There will be opposition, resistance, mistakes, or outright failures, but God has peeled back the future and shown us the ending – and WE WIN! We each win individually, and God has already won for eternity. Think of it this way:

- God created man and the earth and said it was good.
- We are created in God's image.
- God has no lack and his supply never runs out.
- Therefore, we have no lack and God always has exactly what we need to fulfill our calling and assignments.

OK great. What does this have to do with wanting a nice car? My mentor, Natasha Hazlett, uses the phrase, "What I want, wants me". Stick with me for a minute…

When I purchase a car, the salesperson receives a commission for that sale – that is how they make their living. With that money received, he/she cares for their family. The dealership also makes a profit off the sale of a car. They employ people to run the dealership who provide for their families, too. If I want to buy a car and it is reasonable and feasible for me to do so, I am funding families and the economy.

It is OK with God for me to want as nice of a car as I can imagine driving AND it's OK to ask for it. When I am living in alignment with My Creator and I am flowing in the Spirit and I am about my Father's business, the desires of my heart will also be in alignment. If I desire something out of alignment, the Holy Spirit is faithful to nudge me, and I will have a 'check' in my spirit. If there is a green light, I am good to ask with the belief that God will bring the provision for it at exactly the right time. It's my job to stay in alignment, ask within that alignment and then allow God to manage the how and when.

A personal example of "What I want, wants me" is a nudge I have to take a trip to Ireland. Right now I don't see the how or the when, but that trip to Ireland exists in the future that God already knows about. Stay with me again...

When the timing and all the parts and pieces are in position, God will send exactly what I need in the way of money, time, connections, locations, etc. for me to accomplish His plan. I want a trip to Ireland because God has already planned it to happen to accomplish His purpose. That 'purpose' may simply be to bless me, too. I have Irish heritage and have always wanted to visit there. It may or may not be part of a spiritual assignment. Father God loves to bless us the way we love to bless our kids.

Looking back to the future.

Do you remember what you wanted to do and be when you were a kid? There is often truth in those desires because, at that point, we haven't accepted limitations yet. I always saw myself being a teacher. In elementary school, I imagined teaching elementary school because those were the only teachers I knew. As I grew up, I have found myself teaching in many different capacities. One of the personality profiles I took over the years resulted in the categorization of 'Teacher'. No surprise. As a life coach and author, I am also 'teaching' what I have learned to others so writing this book is an example of my childhood dream being a reality.

When we are young, we are close to our authentic self, the real person as God designed us. As we grow and 'mature', we often lose that sense of self in order to 'fit in' and do the things we are supposed to. We are born, already gifted from Heaven with built-in capabilities and talents that God instilled in us while we were in the womb (Psalm 139). Up to about age five, we live in awe and wonder and still carry authenticity. Then we start school and are exposed to the 'norm' and we are expected to conform.

Kids also establish a pecking order – who are the leaders, who are the athletes, who are smart, etc. In my experience and observation, this is where a lot of woundedness begins. We go on through high school and then either enter the job market or go on to more education. That sense of who we were at five years old is often buried under layers of survival. Even having the Lord in your life during these years, life still happens. We live in a world that has continued to move farther away from God's best and we struggle to keep ourselves afloat.

For everyone who experiences any kind of abuse, health issues, accidents, death of a parent or sibling, an addicted parent, narcissistic parent, and many other factors too numerous to list, life has added complications. The fact that you are here now, reading this book is a testimony to you as a survivor and to God's grace in your life. I want to acknowledge you and commend you for your perseverance. I am grateful you are reading this book.

I changed schools between my sophomore and junior years of high school. While I was devastated at the moment of leaving my first school, it was one of the best things that could have happened to me. It gave me a chance to start anew. I was able to take off the facades that had grown comfortable for ten years of going to school with the same kids and take a big step towards really being me. It was hard to start new but again God provided me kids to connect with right away and it eased the transition. With this change, some of my original dreams also returned, or more accurately, re-surfaced.

When I say, "dream big", it will mean something different to every person. When I talk about "playing small", we all have a lot in common. Playing small is a limited mindset. It is filled with phrases like "I can't", "I shouldn't", "That's too big for me", "I don't have the money", "I don't have the talent", or "I don't have ____". Playing small indicates a feeling of scarcity – of not having enough and assuming you don't deserve to ever receive whatever it is you need.

Journey Milestones:

1. What have you been focused on that is NOT what you want? Jot down a list of a few things. Next, reword those things to be the positive version of what you DO want.

_____

_____

_____

_____

_____

_____

2. What is one place in life where you are thinking small? If you are limiting yourself because you don't see the how, give that up to God and write down your hope for His provision and for Him to show His timing.

_____

_____

_____

_____

_____

_____

3. What is a desire of your heart that you have continually shut down in your life because it was too much, or you didn't deserve it? Are you willing to accept that this is something God agrees with you that you can have? Be open to thinking bigger. Write down what comes to your mind now.

_____

_____

_____

_____

_____

_____

Dynamite comes in small packages

In my travels, I met a very special person. Her name is Randi. Randi was born with a health issue. Within the first year of her life, she had to have over a dozen surgeries. Randi is an adult now and to-date has had approximately 60 surgeries – some big, some small. One surgery left her partially blind and prevents her from having peripheral vision on her left side. She walks with the aid of hand crutches and uses a handcycle to get around. None of this has dampened her spirit or her determination to live life on her terms.

Randi recently began participating in snow skiing training with special equipment that empowers disabled people to ski and sled. She inspires me with her courage and determination to overcome her limits and to do so with a Christ-centered attitude. No victim mentality here whatsoever! Randi has not accepted her physical limitations into her mindset or attitude. She has the most let's-go-get-'em spirit I have come across in quite a while. She's now one of my heroes.

I mention her to you for two reasons. First, we do all have physical limits that are real. I will never be a gymnast. My back simply does not bend that way and never has. Also, I am older now – I cannot go back and be 35 again. Physical limitation = truth.

The second reason I told you about Randi is her overcoming spirit and mindset that acknowledges the reality of the physical but doesn't use it as an excuse or an out. She is living her life to the best of her ability and doing everything she can to grow herself. She has learned through repeated experience that God does provide. God has provided medical staff, rides to church, pastors and people to pray for her, finances, experiences, divine contacts at a gym to introduce her to snow sports, and more.

Journey Milestones:

1. Where are you limiting yourself with a mindset that says, "I can't" or "It's not going to work for me"? We build muscles by the repetition of using them – mindset breakthroughs come the same way. Write down your self-imposed limits and then, next to them, write out that you are letting them go and are open to new ideas.

_____

_____

_____

_____

_____

DREAM BIG

As I encourage you to DREAM BIG, I mean it! What do you see yourself doing that is so big that only God could pull it off? Getting a degree, becoming a parent, winning the Iditarod, running a marathon, doing a TED Talk, traveling the world, starting a business, quitting your job to be a stay-at-home parent, paying off your house, buying a nice car, moving to the country, moving to town, living in a foreign country, preaching to hundreds or thousands, getting married, earning a million dollars, etc. Even this list has no bounds. That big thing you might dare to dream about is likely a God-given desire and part of what you were put on earth to accomplish.

Your journey to becoming is unique to you; no one else has the exact same DNA as you or fingerprint as you. You really are the only you. Do not let anyone tell you that you are not enough. You are created exactly as God designed you, as He wanted and needed you to be in order to fill that piece of the puzzle that not one other person in all of time can do. You matter. Your life matters. Your contribution matters. God has kept you alive up until today because you matter. Here's what it looked like for me when I was convinced, I didn't matter.

I remember standing in my closet one day thinking that I needed someone else to live my life for me because I was doing such a poor job of it. At that moment in time, I was ready to outsource my life to someone else. Talk about being in the passenger seat of my own life. I had allowed shame and depression to take the upper hand. I felt out of control and had no clue how to change it. So, I kept putting one foot in front of the other, trudging through life, going to work week after week, fixing meals day after day because I felt trapped. I had bought into the lie that I didn't matter – or if I did matter it was just to make sure everyone else was happy. I let go of my dreams and just existed.

I am happy to report that God intervened! It took a while, but the lie was revealed – another example of God's provision. He brought truth and a reality check. I am by nature a very happy person. My nickname is 'Sunshine' to many of my friends and acquaintances.

However, during this period, my light was pretty dim. The weighty black blanket of shame covered a lot of my light. Just as at night the sun still exists, in the dark period of my life, the light was still there, I just couldn't see it. The same is true for you. You have a light and spark of life within you regardless of what life has thrown at you or thrown on you. God is ready, willing, and able to peel off those layers of darkness to reveal that light within you. I promise it is still there.

This is the essence of what becoming is all about. We describe the un-layering process as 'un-becoming' what you were never designed to be so you can 'be-come' ALL that you were always designed to be.

The processes, exercises, and steps in this book and workbook are all designed to help you tap into your God-given, God-ordained journey to discover the gifts within, identify your BIG DREAMS, confirm your spiritual gifts, and get out of the starting gate. Every single thing you need in the way of provision, wisdom, help, divine appointments, contacts, inventions, creativity – you name it – already exists. That inner nudge you're feeling right now is God as the Holy Spirit prompting you to move forward. Set an intention, take the first step, expect to see the way open before you and you will be amazed at what happens.

Journey Milestone:

1. You have a big dream and you are created for significance. Spend some time thinking bigger and write down every thought and possibility that comes to mind. They may not all come true but be willing to explore what is possible!

_____

_____

_____

_____

_____

_____

Living a chosen life, not life by default.

At different times of my life, I have lived by default. There was no real choice involved. It was going with the flow, taking a day at a time. It wasn't awful but there was no real spark of life either. There were also times when it was bad, hard, and felt hopeless for different reasons. This is not the life that Jesus died on the cross for us to live.

Living life by choice takes more effort and more intentionality and it is far more fulfilling. A chosen life can be looked at in two ways.

First, we are chosen by God to live and serve Him and be in a relationship with him. We also have free will, so the second way is that we live the lifestyle that we have chosen. In neither of these options are we ever a victim. While it is true that every one of us will have hardship and difficulties in life, we always have the choice to control our reaction to whatever comes.

I personally don't thank God *for* the crisis in the midst of the crises; I thank Him for being with me in that circumstance, I can praise Him even during my storm. It is typically sometime after the crisis resolves that I can thank Him for the lessons and what they taught me. I wish there was an easier way to build spiritual fortitude other than going through tough times, but there isn't. You can do and should prepare, but it is only in the real-life moments when toughness hits that we measure our readiness.

And for us as followers of Christ, the best news is, even when we are not prepared, our God is, and He will be our strength and shield and a constant companion through it all. I have experienced it over and over and over where He makes a way where there is no way, "streams in the desert", so to speak. He is faithful beyond what we can even comprehend.

You don't "see" faith being built in yourself. It's built like strata; a little at a time, layer upon layer, and over time it becomes a foundation that you stand on and no one can convince or tell you otherwise because you know.

Journey Milestones:

1. Where have you been living life by default that you need to step up and decide to live with intention?

_____

_____

_____

_____

_____

_____

2. Where have you seen God make a way when it seemed impossible? Let this build and inspire you into more faith.

_____

_____

_____

_____

_____

_____

Conclusion

If I could go back and teach my younger self one principle, it would be to live and design my life with intention AND KEEP DOING IT. I did have intention in choosing what I studied in college, in getting married, in having a child, but I let go of the forward-looking, intentional designing of my life when I gave up and moved into the passenger seat of my own life.

I. Gave. Up.

I allowed myself to become a victim of life's circumstances and it took me down paths that I didn't want to be on.

It is said that when people on their death beds are asked about their greatest regrets, it is the things they didn't do that haunt them.

Do not let perfectionism, fear, self-doubt, insecurity, or the myriad of other excuses we come up with keep you from designing and living your best life. God designed you for a fruitful life, overcoming the obstacles that get in your way, experiencing joy in the struggle, keeping your eye on the prize, blazing new trails, and racking up big and small victories all along the way.

Every one of us is on our own "Journey to Becoming". When you get tired, rest. When you get discouraged, reset your expectations. When you feel like quitting, DON'T!

My all-time favorite quote ever is from Wayne Gretzky,

"You miss 100% of the shots you don't take."

You were fashioned and designed by a miraculous, creative God and He puts His stamp of approval on you. Begin today approving yourself, encouraging yourself, and designing your next adventure on your journey to Becoming Unshakeable.

Bibliography

1. Luft, Joseph, and Ingham, Harrington. *(1955). "The Johari window, a graphic model of interpersonal awareness". Proceedings of the Western Training Laboratory in Group Development. Los Angeles: University of California, Los Angeles.*

2. Carroll, Lewis. Alice in Wonderland, first U.S. edition (the first printing of U.K. edition), 1865

3. Leaf, Dr. Caroline, Switch On Your Brain: The Key to Peak Happiness, Thinking, and Health, 2005

4. New King James Bible, Public Domain, 1987

5. deVenter, Van, I Surrender All, 1896

Invitation to Connect

Today is your day to reconnect with God and move to solid ground. You are God-breathed and God-designed and you have a purpose in this life! God said in the Bible that you are 'fearfully and wonderfully made' (Psalm 139). You are not a mistake. You are intended to be alive right now. We who are here are born and called to such a time as this. We have the life experience, the skills, know-how, and yes, the call on our lives to push forward and overcome whatever life throws at us - - and with God on our side, nothing can stop us.

To keep up with all that is happening with *Becoming Unshakeable*, connect with me at:

Facebook: BecomingUnshakeable – community and group training

Website: http://www.lysabeltz.com/BecomingUnshakeable

Instagram: @CoachLysa

If you want to pursue your journey to Becoming Unshakeable *and* you need help, I am available for you. I offer personal prayer sessions and one-on-one life coaching on my website, **http://www.lysabeltz.com/**. I am also located on Facebook at Women Empowered 4 Life and Instagram at Coach Lysa. You can email me at **CoachLysa@LysaBeltz.com**. I'd love to hear from you.

About the Author

Lysa, an Idaho native, has lived in Boise for most of her life. Lysa spent many years as a programmer/analyst and then project manager in the corporate world. Her ability to build relationships with people and to help them

individually and also as a team served her exceptionally well. She brings that same approach to writing and building relationship with her readers. Her goal is to help you realize your worth and live the life of peace and abundance you were created for.

Lysa has been married to her husband, Scott, for 33 years and has 3 daughters and sons-in-law, grandkids, grand-dogs, and 1 grand-cat. Scott and Lysa also have 3 dogs and a cat of their own, all of whom might be a little spoiled. Currently, all of the kids, pets, grandsons, and grand-animals live in the Boise valley.

Lysa met Jesus when she was 9 years old and has spent a lifetime getting to know Him and His heart for people. She has experienced marriage, divorce, re-marriage, a blended family, the ups and downs of relationships, scarcity, and also abundance. There have been very tough seasons and times of great blessing. Through it all, God has been her foundation and she has seen Him move in ways that can only be described as supernatural. In her books and her life, she uses what she has learned to help any and all that she touches with her faith.

Lysa is known for a warm, caring style and she has a passion to see each person succeed in being the person they were designed to be. Women Empowered 4 Life, the name of her personal empowerment company, perfectly describes Lysa's approach. It's that extra touch of empowerment, plus her ability to hold you accountable in achieving your goals, that makes the partnership so successful and the changes life-impacting.

> *Life is good when you are in the right place, at the right time, doing the right things!*